puppy
school

For Spider, my perfect puppy.

puppy
school

7 steps to the perfect puppy

Gwen Bailey

THUNDER BAY
P·R·E·S·S

San Diego, California

Thunder Bay Press
An imprint of the Advantage Publishers Group
THUNDER BAY 5880 Oberlin Drive, San Diego, CA 92121-4794
P·R·E·S·S www.thunderbaybooks.com

Text copyright © Gwen Bailey 2005
Book design copyright © Octopus Publishing Group Ltd
2005

All notations of errors or omissions should be addressed to
Thunder Bay Press, Editorial Department, at the above address.
All other correspondence (author inquiries, permissions)
concerning the content of this book should be addressed to
Hamlyn, a division of Octopus Publishing Group Ltd, 2–4
Heron Quays, London E14 4JP, England.

Library of Congress Cataloging-in-Publication Data
Bailey, Gwen.
    Puppy school : 7 steps to the perfect puppy / Gwen Bailey.
        p. cm.
    Includes index.
    ISBN-13: 978-1-59223-306-9
    ISBN-10: 1-59223-306-6
    1. Puppies–Training. 2. Puppies–Behavior. 3. Dogs–Training. I. Title.

SF431.B3634 2005
636.7'07--dc22   2004063782

Printed and bound in China
2 3 4 5 09 08 07 06

Introduction 6

Contents

Introduction

This book offers you comprehensive instructions to help you train your puppy to become a well-behaved, happy pet. The step-by-step structured approach will ensure that you and your puppy learn easily and naturally. The methods given are positive and kind and will help you and your puppy to build a wonderful relationship based on love and trust. This book will also help to ensure that your puppy will grow up to be sociable and confident with people, reducing the chances that he will resort to aggression as an adult.

All puppies are different. Their genetic makeup, combined with the different experiences they have had, will give them a unique set of characteristics. This variation gives each puppy his own set of built-in traits and preferences, making some puppies easier to train and raise than others. For this reason, the training program has been designed to be flexible so that you can go at a speed that is appropriate to your puppy. It doesn't matter if it takes six weeks or sixty, as long as you are making progress all the time. If you are experiencing difficulties or have a puppy who seems difficult to teach, get professional help early on rather than waiting until problems have become long-established habits.

The training techniques featured in this book are recommended for puppies between the ages of three and five months old. They are suitable for dogs and puppies of all ages, but it may take you a bit longer to achieve results if your puppy is older, as it is likely that he will have already learned some unwanted actions. If your puppy is excessively shy, you will need to go more slowly so that you do not overwhelm him with too much at once.

Good training and education during your puppy's first year will help him to grow into a well-trained, well-adjusted dog. It is possible for all puppies to grow up to be like this, but whether they do or not depends on how much effort is made by their owners. Time and care spent while your puppy is still young enough to mold to your ways will be well rewarded. Try to make sure that you do a little every day, and have fun so that training doesn't become a chore. In no time at all, with the help of this book, you will have a well-behaved adult dog who can be taken everywhere and who is a pleasure to own.

Note:
Puppies are referred to as "he" throughout to avoid "he/she" or the rather impersonal "it." The use of the pronoun reflects no bias towards males; both sexes are equally valuable and as easy to train.

Starting off well

Start off well, encouraging your puppy to do the right thing while preventing or stopping unwanted behavior. Getting it right from the beginning is much easier for both of you.

It may take a few months for your puppy to learn how to live successfully with humans and to adjust fully to his new surroundings, so don't expect too much too soon. Formal training can wait for a few weeks until your puppy has settled in, but good habits can be started right way.

To teach a puppy how to behave well, you need to be there to supervise him. During your puppy's first year, look after him when he is in the house and yard, and encourage him to behave in an acceptable way so that he can be praised and rewarded.

If your puppy has already started an unwanted behavior, stop him immediately, show him what he should be doing, and praise him when he does so. Since he may have already found out how much fun the unwanted behavior was, you need to watch carefully to prevent him from repeating it.

Remember to reward good behavior when it happens naturally with praise, games, and treats. It is easy to forget about your puppy when he is being well behaved, but try to remember to reward him so that he is encouraged to be good more often.

GOOD MANNERS

When most owners start out with a puppy, they hope they will be able to look after it its whole life. Sadly, this is not always possible and dogs do sometimes need to be found new homes.

To make sure that your puppy has a good chance of finding a new home easily if the need should arise, try to raise him in such a way that his behavior will be acceptable anywhere. You may not mind if he jumps up, sleeps on the bed, hates children, bites the towel while being dried, or is aggressive over his food, but others may find this more difficult to deal with. To make him easier to live with and to make him into a dog that anyone would be happy to own, it is a good idea to try to iron out any problems and to teach him good manners while he is still a puppy. If you can manage to accomplish this now while he is still young, then good behavior will come naturally to him as he grows.

Q&As

Q Where should I put my puppy when I am unable to supervise him?

A A puppy playpen will prevent your puppy from getting into mischief and learning bad habits when you are not there to supervise him.

Q What sort of playpen should I get and how large should it be?

A The pen needs to be secure and big enough to have separate areas for sleeping and playing.

Q How long should he spend in the playpen?

A Make sure that your puppy is in the pen for short periods only and never for longer than one hour.

Q My puppy is reluctant to go in his playpen. How can I get him to go in without forcing him?

A Encourage him to go there with a few treats when he is tired and needs to rest.

Q What should I put in the playpen?

A Cover the floor of the playpen first with plastic, then with a layer of newspaper. Always give your puppy a chance to go to the bathroom before confining him in his pen. Leave him some water in a small bowl and some toys and chews, and make sure that he has a comfortable bed to rest on.

TIPS FOR SUCCESS

- Try to prevent unwanted behavior by thinking ahead so that he never learns how rewarding it can be to do the wrong thing.

- Put things you don't want him to have out of reach and block off access to cords and other dangerous items that he may chew.

- Provide him with lots of things he can play with and explore instead.

Building a good relationship

A good relationship between you and your puppy is essential if he is to be well behaved and well adjusted. A relationship based on friendship and trust will ensure that he tries hard to win your praise and approval, thereby making it more likely that he will want to do as you ask.

The bond will take time to build and is not something that can be created overnight. Young puppies need to learn how to understand and communicate with humans, who are, after all, members of a different species. However, safe in the knowledge that you will be fair and treat him well, a consistent, kind, and thoughtful approach during your puppy's first year will enable him to learn easily.

Play helps to build and strengthen the bond between owner and puppy. Puppies don't automatically know how to play games with humans, having grown up playing with other puppies in the litter by biting and mouthing. Until they learn, they will try to play with us in a similar way by biting our hands, feet, and any part of us that moves quickly. Since this is an unacceptable type of play to most people and particularly so to children or elderly people, who tend to have thinner skin, it is important that we teach them how to enjoy playing games with toys instead.

Puppies will try to play their favorite game when they get excited. Offer a toy at a time when your puppy is excited by someone coming home, when you approach him after an absence, or at any other times when he is eager to do something.

Make it exciting by keeping the toy moving and letting him get it sometimes. Try to have fun and concentrate on the toy and the game rather than on the puppy. Different puppies prefer different games, so experiment with chase games, tug games, or games with squeaky toys to see which your puppy prefers.

Play energetically, but stop immediately and walk away if the games get too rough or if your puppy accidentally bites your hands. In this way, he will learn to be gentle in his games and will try to avoid putting his teeth on human skin.

A HAPPY PARTNERSHIP

A relationship based on love and trust is the best foundation for an easy and rewarding life with your puppy. Positive training, plenty of games with toys, and the meeting of all his needs will ensure a contented, well-behaved puppy that works hard to please you.

TIPS FOR SUCCESS

• Play often, choosing spare moments in your day such as while the coffee is brewing or during commercials. Keep a toy out of reach of your puppy in each room of the house and replace it after the game so that there is always a toy easily available and you do not have to go looking for one.

• Play with him regularly. This will help to use up your puppy's excess energy, making him easier to live with. As well as using up physical energy, playing will also help to tire him mentally so that he is calmer.

• Playing with your puppy will make him more focused on you, encouraging a better bond to form between you and him. This will help with his training.

• Use soft toys that your puppy can bite easily. Hard plastic toys are difficult to find and can be painful for teething puppies.

WHEN IT GOES WRONG

There will be times when events or your puppy's behavior make you angry or frustrated. It is natural, although not advisable, to take it out on your puppy. Provided these are isolated incidents in an otherwise usually calm sea of emotions, your puppy will be able to take them in stride. Using the positive training techniques in this book, you will be able to to tell your puppy what you want him to do. This will help to reduce confusion and frustration and will allow you to have a more harmonious relationship with your puppy, particularly during the difficult time of adolescence.

• A good relationship is built on love and trust.

• Remember, your puppy does not speak English.

• It takes time to build a working partnership.

What to do about play biting

Play biting is just your puppy's way of trying to get you to play with him. In the litter, he would have excitedly run at other puppies and bitten them to encourage them to play. The other puppies would have responded and bitten back, and a happy rough-and-tumble game would then have begun. So it is perfectly natural for a puppy to try to get us to play in the same way.

Unlike his siblings, however, we have thin skin and no fur, and when puppies bite us with their sharp teeth, it hurts. Therefore, it is important to teach your puppy to play more appropriate games by teaching him to play with toys.

At first, he will think that games with toys are a poor substitute for rough-and-tumble biting games. However, if these are the only games that are allowed, your puppy will soon catch on and begin to enjoy the way you play.

Until your puppy has learned not to bite humans, have a toy ready whenever you interact with him. Offer the toy so that it can be bitten instead of you, and keep it wriggling enticingly so that your puppy is attracted to it. If your puppy bites you instead, try to keep that part of your body still and attract him back to the toy by

wriggling it furiously. The less you react when your puppy bites, the quicker he will learn how unrewarding it is. When he bites on the toy, encourage and praise him and play exciting games. This will quickly teach him to bite on toys and to play with humans via toys instead.

MORE CONTROL

If your puppy is older and stronger and is still play biting or your puppy bites at you as you move away, attach a lead to his collar and use this to prevent him from reaching you. Allow him closer to you only when he is biting the toy; otherwise, move him away to a safe distance using the line. This technique is particularly useful for teaching puppies that children are not substitute littermates, even though they are lively, fun and closer to their size than adults.

TIPS FOR SUCCESS

• Be gentle when playing tug games, as your puppy may be losing teeth and may have a sore mouth at times.

• Remember that it takes time for puppies to learn to play successfully with humans. Be patient and keep showing him how to play fun games with toys.

BEATING BITING

If you have children, you are elderly, or you have a puppy that bites very hard and it is impossible to ignore the bites, you will need to let your puppy know that he is hurting you.

• To do this, say "ouch" loudly as soon as you have been bitten, stand up slowly, and move away. This will help your puppy to learn that hard bites result in the end of a game and a loss of social contact. Eventually he will learn to be more careful.

• Supervise young children carefully when they play with your puppy and stop any games that involve the puppy biting on skin or clothes.

• Teach both parties how to play successfully with toys instead.

Children and dogs in the family

If you have children, it is important that your puppy learns to interact with them safely and appropriately. Left to their own devices, both may treat the other as a toy, behaving in a way that encourages misbehavior and bad habits.

Because both children and puppies are young and inexperienced, it is necessary for an adult to supervise interactions at all times. This may seem unnecessary, but it is better to put in the time and effort early to ensure that good habits are created, rather than to try to sort out problems later.

First impressions are important, so it is a good idea to get the children to sit down when a new puppy is brought in for the first time. They can be given small treats to offer on the flat of their hands when the puppy comes to investigate them.

Once the puppy is used to the children, teach them how to play together successfully with toys. Show the children how to handle the puppy gently once he is used to being touched all over by adults.

OTHER DOGS IN THE FAMILY

If you have another dog in the family or are trying to raise two puppies together, it is really important that the puppy plays more with humans than he does with the other dog or puppy. This is because the familiar game of rough-and-tumble biting with other dogs is more fun than learning to play with humans. Although it is nice to see your puppy playing with other dogs, if this is allowed in excess, he will form a strong bond with other dogs and less of a bond with you. As a result, he will be less focused on you and much more difficult to train. This may also result in him growing into an adult dog who cannot be recalled from games with other dogs in the park.

Q&As

Q How do I keep the puppy from learning how to beg at the table?

A Use stair gates or a playpen to confine the puppy while children eat so that the puppy does not learn to pester or beg for food.

Q What can I do to ensure that things don't get out of hand in my absence?

A When you cannot be there to supervise, place the puppy in his playpen so that he can rest and learn to amuse himself rather than learning to chase or bite the children in an unsupervised situation.

Q How should my children offer treats to the puppy?

A They should hold their hands flat, keeping their fingers and thumb close together so that the puppy can take the treat without risk of biting their hands accidentally. It is best to teach the children how to do this before the puppy arrives.

Q I don't have a child, but I want my puppy to get used to children. What should I do?

A It is important that your puppy learns to interact with different ages of children as soon as possible. Follow the guidelines on socialization (see pages 36–37) to ensure that he grows up to be well adjusted and able to enjoy and tolerate their company when he is older.

TIPS FOR SUCCESS

• To ensure that your puppy grows up to be human-focused and nicer to own, make certain that he plays with people roughly three times longer than he plays with other dogs. So, for example, if he plays for five minutes with other dogs, you need to play with him for up to fifteen minutes (in short sessions).

• Restrict his access to the other dogs/puppies in your household unless you are there to supervise and encourage them to play with you rather than each other. Use a stair gate or playpen to ensure that this happens.

• By playing with him frequently and by keeping his attention on you, he will be easier to train and a nicer dog to own.

• If you own more than one dog, take your puppy out and about without your adult dog so that he becomes independent and confident when alone.

House-training

All animals born in a nest can be house-trained, as they are naturally preprogrammed to keep their bed clean. All you have to do is teach your puppy that the whole of your house is his nest.

It is possible to house-train a puppy very quickly. The secret lies in being very vigilant (puppies have immature brains and bodies and can't hold on for long) and taking your puppy out regularly to the place where he should go to the bathroom. Keep an eye on him when he is loose in the house. Always know where he is and what he is up to. If he begins to circle and sniff the ground, starts to whine, walks around looking uncomfortable, or looks as though he is concentrating with a faraway look in his eyes, take him outside. When puppies feel the need to go, they need to go outside quickly, so don't delay.

Go out with him, even if it is raining. Allow him to run around and sniff, as both of these actions will help him relax and make it more likely that he will go to the bathroom. Praise him gently when he begins to go.

Stay outside with him even if it is cold and raining. If you are not there to watch him, he will turn his attention to getting back into the safety of the house and will still need to go when you let him back in.

When visitors arrive, it is easy to forget about your puppy's needs, but the excitement of greeting new people may cause him to need to relieve himself, so remember to take him out to the yard as soon as things have settled down.

YOU NEED TO TAKE YOUR PUPPY OUT
- after he eats
- after he's been playing
- after any excitement
- after he's been sleeping or resting
- every one to two hours

HOW QUICKLY?

If you keep to this schedule and you are patient and vigilant enough, your puppy should be house-trained within a few weeks and certainly by the time he is six months old. However, some puppies take longer to house-train than others, so don't expect too much too soon. Their young brains will take time to learn what is required and it will be a while before they have full control over their bodies. Don't expect them to be completely clean before they are six months old, particularly at nighttime when they may have to wait for many hours before they are able to get outside.

If you cannot be with him or you cannot concentrate on him, put him in a puppy playpen, large enough for his bed and a bathroom area covered with plastic and newspaper. Then if he needs to go when you are not there, he will not get into the habit of soiling the house. As soon as you are free, take him outside.

Q&As

Q **Why has my puppy had an accident after being clean for some time?**
A It takes time to learn good habits, so expect accidents to happen and consider it your failure for not supervising him properly rather than his inability to learn.

Q **What should I do if I see him going to the bathroom in the house?**
A Try not to get upset, but hurry him out to the yard, stay out with him until he has finished what he started, and then shut him in another room while you clear up the mess.

Q **What is the best way to clean up the mess?**
A Clean up any accidents with detergent and carpet cleaner. Allow to dry and apply stain remover if necessary. Careful cleaning will get rid of the smell that may otherwise attract him back to that area next time.

TIPS FOR SUCCESS

• At nighttime, take his playpen upstairs so that he can be confined but you can hear him if he wakes up and needs to go to the bathroom.

• When you hear him moving around, take him out right away and wait with him, even if it is cold, dark, and raining. He will be house-trained more quickly if you do this.

• Do not give him attention at nighttime unless he goes to the bathroom or you may find that he learns to get you out of bed whenever he is lonely or wants company.

Teaching "off"

It is useful to teach your puppy that "off" means "take your face and body away from what you are interested in and you will be rewarded." This exercise is easy to teach and can be used if, for example, your puppy is getting too close to food on a low table or is biting your fingers too hard.

Your puppy needs to learn that humans always get their own way and that it is easier to give in to them sooner rather than later. For this reason, if you are in a position to ensure that it happens, ask your puppy to do something, even if he doesn't want to do it.

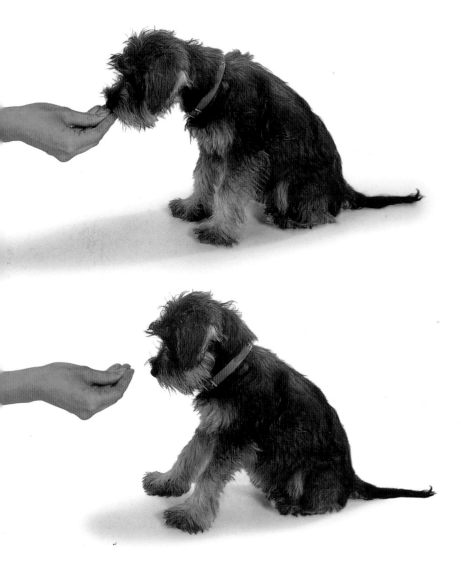

1 Give your puppy a treat. Hold another up, say "off," and keep it held tightly between your thumb and finger. Allow your puppy to lick, chew, and paw at your hand, but ignore this behavior. Be patient, keep your hand still, and wait until you see a space appear between your hand and your puppy's nose, then feed the treat immediately.

2 Repeat until your puppy learns that when you say "off," he needs to take his face away to get the treat. Practice this in several sessions until he will move his head away as soon as you say "off." Then gradually build up the time he can wait until you can count to ten before rewarding. Practice in different locations and situations.

TIPS FOR SUCCESS

• Keep your hand very still when you say "off."

• At first, give the treat **as soon as** you see a gap appear between your hand and your puppy's nose.

• Only say "off" once and then keep quiet and wait for your puppy to take his face away.

• When you use the "off" for a real-life event, such as if your puppy is about to take something off the table, reward him for responding and find him an extra-tasty treat to reinforce his good behavior.

• If your puppy bites or scratches your fingers too hard, wear an old leather glove while you teach "off." When you take the glove off, you will need to teach him again, but this time it should be faster and less painful.

Q&As

Q My puppy won't do what I want. How should I discipline him?

A There is no need to discipline, shout at, or punish your puppy, but, on occasion, you will need to be strong-willed about making him behave as you wish. This will help your puppy to learn to deal with the feelings of frustration that will inevitably occur when he does not get his own way.

Q When should I start to insist on getting my own way?

A All puppies—and humans—need to learn how to deal with the feeling generated when they cannot get their own way, and it is easier to teach them this when they are little rather than when they are bigger and stronger.

Q What do I do if he gets upset or barks at me?

A If your puppy cannot get his own way and begins to get upset or bark, continue to prevent him from doing what he wants until he relaxes, then reward him well.

SETTING BOUNDARIES

Setting boundaries for your puppy will result in a compliant, amenable dog who is very easy to live with. Always insist, gently but firmly, that your puppy does what you want, such as not climbing on the sofa, so he learns that there is no point in trying to resist.

Remember to make it very rewarding for him once he does what you have asked.

Chewing

Chewing is a natural and normal activity for puppies. It is important to appreciate the different stages and to provide plenty of appropriate items for them to chew in order to prevent them from damaging valuable items.

Puppies lose their deciduous teeth between four and six months of age and then begin to grow their larger adult teeth. During this time, they will chew a lot to help ease the discomfort in their mouths, just as babies do. Puppies also chew as a way of investigating objects in their surroundings, in much the same way as toddlers use their hands.

There are lots of chews on the market, so buy a selection and put a few different ones down for your puppy each day, picking up those that have been down for a while. This will help to keep the chews novel and interesting for your puppy. When you need to leave him, put him in a puppy playpen with a few chews and toys he has not seen for a while so that he does not chew things he should not during your absence.

Providing your puppy with strong items that would otherwise be thrown away, such as cardboard boxes or thick plastic bottles, will give him a chance to use his jaws, reducing the need to give him items bought from a pet store. Encourage him to investigate these items by placing tasty treats inside them. Give these to him only when you are there to watch him and remove any pieces that may be swallowed or harmful.

KEEPING HIM OCCUPIED

Toys can, occasionally, be stuffed with tasty food, such as cream cheese, peanut butter or pieces of cheese and meat. Stuffed toys can occupy a puppy for quite a while, allowing you to continue with important jobs. It can also help to orient him to toys when he feels the urge to chew next time.

ADOLESCENT CHEWING

Puppies of some breeds will chew more than others. Gundogs, especially Labradors, have been selected over generations for an ability to use their mouths and will be particularly prone to chewing during their first year.

During adolescence, from about six to 12 months, your puppy is likely to chew more, and as he is larger, this will enable him to do more damage. Be prepared for this.

• Treat him in the same way as you did when he was teething so that he does not destroy anything valuable.

• To help you and your puppy get through this phase, give him lots of physical and mental exercise, and make sure that he has plenty of opportunity to explore away from home.

• Give him a good variety of things to chew each day.

TIPS FOR SUCCESS

• Offering your puppy plenty of things to chew should satisfy his desire to exercise his jaws and keep his interest. This will make it less likely that he will chew things he should not.

• Your puppy was not born knowing right from wrong, so it is important that you are there to supervise and teach him. Make sure that you pay attention to him when you are with him and distract him from chewing anything that you do not want him to chew.

• Put away things that are valuable or dangerous so that he cannot get them.

• Make it easy for him to chew what you want him to chew and encourage him and praise him for doing the right thing.

Problem solver

All puppy owners, however experienced, encounter problems from time to time. These sections at the end of every chapter give solutions to the most common difficulties that you are likely to face. For more difficult problems, ask advice from behaviorists, trainers, and experienced friends.

Problem 1

My five-month-old puppy makes a mess in the kitchen every night.

Puppies take time to learn to control their bodies and you shouldn't expect a puppy to be completely clean until he is six months old. However, you will need to teach your puppy to be clean at night.

• Consider taking him into your bedroom at night, confining him to a small area so that you can hear him when he wakes up and moves around.

• Take him outside and stay with him so that you can praise him when he goes to the bathroom (failing to do this every time will prolong the time it takes for him to learn).

• Once he has been clean all night for two weeks, you can return him to the kitchen. Clean the floor thoroughly before you do so (see page 17) to prevent any lingering smells that may encourage him to return to his old habits.

Problem 2

Our new puppy isn't interested in playing, despite all our attempts to encourage him, and he seems to be frightened of the toys.

Some puppies who have not had much chance to interact with humans while in the litter may be shy and a little nervous around humans. Your puppy may need more time to get to know you before he feels relaxed enough to risk playing.

• Encourage him to feel safe by being gentle and considerate, and roll toys away from him without getting close and pressuring him into playing.

• When he feels more comfortable with humans, you should notice that he gets playful when he gets excited. Take this opportunity to produce soft, inviting toys and play gently. Try putting some tasty pieces of food inside a toy to attract him to it.

• Remember to keep things fun and concentrate on the toy rather than the puppy.

YOUR PUPPY'S NAME

Your puppy will quickly learn to pay attention to you when he hears his name if you call it whenever you have something nice to give to him. After a while, your puppy will begin to look at you to see what is going to happen when you say it.

Once he is responding to his name, you can use it to get him to look at you just before you ask him to do something during the training exercises. There is no need to say his name if he is already looking at you and paying attention—just use it at times when he is looking in a different direction or has his mind on other things.

SIGNALS AND WORDS

Everyone in the family should decide on which signals and words will be used to ask for particular actions. Always use the same signals and cues to save confusion and speed up training.

Action	Voice cue (Write your chosen voice cue on the dotted line)	Hand signal
Sit _____	....	
Down _____	....	
Stand _____	....	
Wait _____	....	
Come when called _____	....	
Walk on loose lead _____	....	

Reward-based training

Reward-based training is much kinder and more effective for puppies and owners than the outdated techniques that relied on punishment. Rewards make training fun, and will not only help to strengthen your relationship with your puppy, but will make your puppy want to behave well.

To train effectively, you need something that excites your puppy. While puppies are still young, praise from owners can be exciting. However, since most puppies are used to getting affection all the time from their owners, something extra is needed to encourage them to work hard enough to learn the exercises. Find out what motivates your puppy by trying the exercises shown in Getting Attention (see pages 26–27) and use whatever he is most interested in. Once you have his full attention, training will be easier.

You don't need any special equipment to train your puppy other than a plain buckle collar and a lead. Avoid collars and leads made of chain, as these will hurt your puppy's neck or your hands.

Check that the collar fits well and that you can slip two fingers under it. Make sure also that it is tight enough not to pull over your puppy's head so that he cannot get out of it when you are in an unsafe place. Continue to check the fit of the collar as your puppy grows. Attach an identification tag to it in case he gets lost.

Good timing is critical if your puppy is to learn easily. Always reward as soon as your puppy does the right thing so that he learns that the reward came for performing that particular action.

USING TOYS

Some puppies, especially older ones, work harder for a game with a toy than for food. Soft toys that can be bitten and tugged are best. The disadvantage of using toys is that they are not always easy to use as a lure. You also have to let go of the toy to use it as a reward and get it back again afterward, which is not always as quick and easy as feeding a treat. However, if you have a puppy that prefers toys to treats, you should use games as a reward for training. Keep a favorite toy for this purpose so that it is always of interest to your puppy.

Q&As

Q What treats should I give my puppy?
A There are plenty of tasty treats on the market that can be broken up into small pieces.

Q He does not seem interested in commercial treats. Can I use anything else?
A Cooked liver, which has been cut into small cubes and dried in the oven, and cheese are usually very acceptable to puppies (only feed small amounts of liver; save it for difficult exercises).

Q Can I give him bits of his food as treats?
A Soft, smelly food is usually more acceptable than dry, hard food, but some puppies will work well for the dry kibble food they are usually fed.

Q I tried to give my puppy a new food as a treat, but it upset his stomach. Does this mean that I should always keep him on the same food?
A If you are introducing new foods, be careful not to feed too much too soon, upsetting his digestion. Gradually increase amounts in the early days of training so that he gets used to it slowly.

Q Will my puppy get fat if I feed him treats?
A Don't let your puppy get too fat as a result of feeding lots of treats. The best way to avoid this is to measure out his daily amount of food, replace some with special treats for training, and make sure that the food and treats form a balanced diet (ask your vet for advice about this).

TIPS FOR SUCCESS

• Use the treats that work best for your puppy. You may find that, after a few weeks, your puppy begins to lose interest in working for familiar treats, so vary them from week to week.

• Don't try to train your puppy soon after a meal. He needs to be interested in working for the treats you are offering during training, so he needs to be hungry during lessons.

• Don't try to train him when he is really hungry, as this could affect his ability to concentrate.

• Treats should be small so that your puppy does not become full too quickly. Pieces about the size of a pea are best.

Getting attention

If your puppy is to learn anything you are trying to teach, he must be paying attention to you. These games will help to teach your puppy to focus on you for long enough so that you are able to teach him the lessons he needs to learn.

The following games will help you to learn how to get your puppy's full attention. This is important if you are going to train him successfully, as you will need him to be completely focused on you before you begin each exercise. Practice these games and then use them to help get your puppy in the mood to learn as well as focusing him on you before the start of each session.

Tail-wagging game
See how much you can make your puppy's tail wag. Who in the family can make the puppy's tail wag the most? What do they do that can be copied by everyone? What makes your puppy pay most attention? Be silly, have fun, and offer treats, games, and praise in a high-pitched, excited voice. Rub him lightly and quickly along his sides, clap, move around, and generally act like a fool! The more excitement you can generate, the more your puppy's tail will wag and the more attention you will have, which will help with his training.

Look-at-me game
Show your puppy that you have something he wants, say his name, hold it under your chin, and wait until he looks up at you. Then give the treat or have a game with the toy. Repeat over several sessions until your puppy looks at you whenever you say his name. Once you are getting eye contact easily when you say your puppy's name, gradually increase the length of time you hold his attention. Start slowly, counting to two before rewarding, then repeat counting to three before rewarding and so on.

IN THE MOOD TO LEARN

As well as being interested in food or wanting to play, your puppy also needs to be alert and lively rather than tired. Choose times for training during the day when he has had enough rest, when he does not have to go to the bathroom, and when he is not distracted by anything else. If you own a boisterous puppy who has lots of energy, try to arrange a vigorous play and free-running session in a safe place before training. This will help to ensure that your puppy is in a calm, ready-to-learn mood.

$Q\&A$s

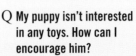

Q **My puppy isn't interested in me when I try to play with him. What can I do?**
A Relax, have fun, be silly!

Q **My puppy isn't interested in any toys. How can I encourage him?**
A Try moving the toys about rapidly and erratically (imitate a small, moving animal). Let your puppy have the toy to play with more often.

Q **My puppy looks everywhere but in my eyes. Is he afraid of me?**
A Some puppies are shy and don't like to stare at their owners. Reward even a glance or a near miss so that you encourage and eventually build up the behavior you want.

Q **My puppy gets distracted easily when I am playing with him. What can I do?**
A Try again in a quieter area. Make sure that you have something the puppy really wants.

Q **My puppy tries to avoid being touched. How can I help him overcome this?**
A Be gentler with your hands and go slower. Stroke, rather than pat along his sides, and avoid the sensitive head area.

GOLDEN RULES FOR TRAINING
- Aim to succeed every time.
- Practice each exercise several times a day.
- Work in short sessions of less than three minutes.
- Finish each session on a positive note.

Coming back when called

Coming back when called is one of the most important things that we need to teach our puppies. If a dog comes back when called, he can be let off the lead to play and use up energy, resulting in a well-exercised pet who is calmer and easier to live with. Teaching a quick response to our calls may also save a dog's life if he is heading for danger.

Begin teaching the recall as soon as you can while your puppy is still very young and is still very interested in being with you. As puppies mature and go through adolescence, their attention turns to the outside world, and it will be harder to train them to do this exercise.

1 Teach this exercise in your house and yard where your puppy can be safely off the lead. Get someone to hold your puppy. Show him that you have a reward, step backward, and crouch down.

2 Ask your helper to release your puppy when you call. Call your puppy.

3 When he gets to you, reward him well with plenty of praise and a treat or game with a toy. Repeat several times, gradually increasing the distance between both of you.

Call him for things he likes, such as going for a walk or giving him his dinner, and practice up to twenty times a day for many weeks so that this lesson is learned well.

Once your puppy has learned to come when you call, try this exercise when he is busy elsewhere in the house or yard so that he learns to come to you whatever he is doing.

Q&As

Q My puppy isn't interested in coming to me. What should I do?

A Make sure that you have something he wants. Be light-hearted, relax, and have fun so that you don't put too much pressure on your puppy. Don't go too far away at first so that it is easy for your puppy to get to you. Try again in a quieter, less-distracting area.

Q My puppy is not coming right up to me. Is he scared of me?

A Don't pat or touch his head when he comes to you. Some shy puppies are overwhelmed by staring and calling, so try turning to the side, looking away from your puppy, and calling gently. You may have tried to grab your puppy in the past and he has learned to avoid you. Be patient, hold out the treat, and lure him in toward you. Stroke him gently as he eats the treat, but don't grab him.

TIPS FOR SUCCESS

• Use a high-pitched, happy voice and offer him something he really wants.

• When your puppy gets to you, slip a finger into his collar before feeding him the treat so that he remains with you for the next practice. Make sure that you put your hand under his head when you do this, as reaching above his head may make him back away.

LEARNING HANDLING SKILLS

It will take time for you to learn the handling skills needed to make the training exercises in this book work successfully, particularly if this is your first puppy. Learning how to hold the treat, how to use it as a lure, how to hold your puppy, how to use the lead to prevent unwanted behavior, and how to acquire the other skills you need takes practice. If you are new to puppy training, don't expect to be good at it to begin with. Keep practicing and you will get better.

Getting used to being handled

Humans like to touch, hold, and hug when showing affection, whereas dogs rarely come into contact with each other unless they are fighting or mating. Your puppy needs to get used to being handled, and if you are gentle, trustworthy, and persistent, he will also learn to enjoy it.

Teaching dogs to be handled is also necessary for when there is something wrong with them and they need to be examined. A trusting dog that is used to being touched, restrained, and gently manipulated will be a much better patient and will be more likely to get better, quicker treatment compared with one that gets defensive or aggressive.

In addition, other people who like dogs will often assume that your dog is friendly and will touch him without asking. Since it is essential that dogs are not aggressive, it is important to prepare him for all the things that adults and children might do to him in order to ensure that he takes it all in his stride and does not get worried.

1 Begin slowly, holding him firmly so that he cannot wriggle free. Gradually touch and stroke him, working along his back, from his head down his front legs to the paws, under his belly, and down his back legs and tail.

2 Go at a speed that he can deal with, letting him get used to slow, gentle touching on one part of his body before moving on to the next. Use treats to keep his mind occupied while you touch sensitive areas.

3 Practice drying him with a small towel, moving it slowly at first so that he does not get excited and try to bite at it. Begin in small stages, letting him go after he has accepted a few wipes at first and gradually build this up. If your puppy bites at the towel, move it more slowly and hold his collar to prevent him from doing so while you run it over the back end of his body.

TIPS FOR SUCCESS

• Get down to his level at first so that he can stand or sit on the floor rather than having to be lifted up.

• Make sure that your fingers are not digging into him when you hold him.

• Talk to him softly while you handle him.

• If you find a sensitive area, go there slowly and gradually until he accepts it.

• Practice regularly and at least once a day.

4 Get your puppy used to being hugged. After hugging him, give him a treat or play a game so that he learns to enjoy the experience.

TROUBLESHOOTING CHECKLIST ✓

If your puppy gets very excited, struggles and wriggles, play bites, or gets aggressive when you hold him:

• Slow everything down even more.

• Talk to him in a slow, soothing way.

• Keep your hand movements slow.

• Try to hold him in such a way that he cannot wriggle free or hurt you, but don't squeeze him too tightly. The more secure your hold, the sooner he will relax.

• Practice holding him firmly many times a day. Wait until he relaxes and then let him free at once. He will soon learn that calm behavior buys his freedom more quickly than struggling.

5 When lifting your puppy, use one hand under his chest to control his movement and support his weight with the other hand under his bottom. If your puppy struggles when being lifted, don't lift him up too fast—it will give him the same feeling as when you go up too fast in a elevator. Get down to his level and bring him into your body as soon as his legs leave the floor so that he feels secure.

Car travel

Car travel is a necessary part of human existence and it is important for dogs to get used to traveling in cars from an early age. Failure to do this can result in a dog that barks, jumps around, or chews in the car, which might lead you to leave him at home rather than having him accompany the rest of the family on their travels.

Being in a car is not a natural experience for a young puppy and can be unsettling, so it is important to acclimatize him slowly. Begin as soon as your puppy has had a chance to settle into your household by taking him on small journeys at first and gradually

extending them. Try to take him somewhere every day during the first few months, even though you may not always take him out of the car until you get back home. In this way, he will soon get used to car travel and accept it as a necessary part of life.

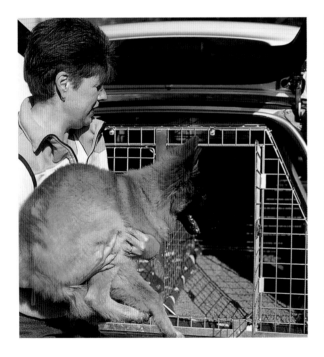

Place your puppy somewhere in the car where he will be safe and where his movement will be restricted so that he does not learn to jump around and distract the driver. If he is to travel on the seat, use a car harness so that he cannot fall off. Good use can be made of a travel cage to ensure that he remains safe, but get him used to being confined in it at home first and make sure that it is big enough for him to stand up, turn around, and lie down.

Later, you can teach your puppy to stay in the car while the doors are opened so that he stays safe until you are ready for him to get out (see page 109). When you reach your destination, give him a short walk or a short play session.

Q&As

Q **My puppy is frightened of being in the car; he dribbles, drools, and is car sick. Can I cure this?**

A Take your puppy on many very short journeys, never going farther than he can deal with at one time without stopping. For some puppies, this may mean taking them repeatedly to the end of the road and then driving slowly home. Gradually accustoming your puppy to traveling in this way may take a long time at first, but it will be well worth it in the end, as you will have a dog who is happy to travel and can be taken anywhere.

Q **My puppy jumps up at the windows and barks as things go past. I am worried that he may hurt himself. How do I stop him?**

A You will need to confine your puppy so that he cannot see things that are going past outside. This will teach him to settle down in the car and rest rather than learning to have fun trying to chase things that go past at high speed.

TIPS FOR SUCCESS

• Place your puppy on soft, nonslip, absorbent bedding for the journey.

• Close doors carefully without slamming and don't start the car until the puppy is inside, as the exhaust can be frightening and unpleasant.

• Drive considerately. Remember that your puppy cannot see where the car is going, is not supported by a seat, and cannot predict when the next corner will be coming up. Take corners and bends at a slow speed and accelerate and decelerate smoothly.

• Corners and bends cause the car to move unpredictably from your puppy's point of view. When traveling long distances with your puppy, try to find routes that involve straight roads such as freeways, especially if he is car sick.

• Feed him small meals in the car when it is stationary to give pleasant associations with being inside.

Learning to be alone

Many dogs get anxious about being left alone and show unwanted behavior such as barking, chewing, or going to the bathroom in the house. Being isolated is not a comfortable situation for a sociable pack animal, particularly one that is very young and vulnerable. Puppies need to learn gradually to deal with the uncomfortable feelings that isolation creates.

It is quite easy to teach a puppy to accept being left alone, as long as it is done slowly and carefully. Some insecure puppies may not feel completely confident about being alone until they reach maturity, but they will cope much better if the process is begun early.

Teaching puppies to accept isolation is particularly important if you have a busy family and there isn't always someone around. There may come a time in your dog's life when he cannot be with people and it is better that he learns to cope while he is young rather than when he is an adult. It is also important that your puppy learns to be alone if you have another dog in the family. Dogs that have always had the company of others can find it very difficult to manage alone if their companion should die before them, so it is worth making the effort needed to teach him to be independent.

Once your puppy feels comfortable with the family and has found his way around the house, begin to leave him in another room occasionally for just a few minutes. Wait until he is tired and give him a comfortable bed to sleep on. After a few minutes, open the door and let him come out if he wants to. Repeat this exercise, gradually, over many weeks, leaving him for longer periods of time until he can deal with being left alone for an hour.

If he shows distress at any time by frantically barking or scratching at the door, leave him for a shorter time next time and progress more slowly. Once he is happy to be left in one room, teach him again in other rooms throughout the house.

TAKING IT FURTHER

When he is happy to be left alone in any room of the house, you will need to repeat the whole procedure, but this time leave the house. The procedure will take less time if you have taught him well in the house.

Q&As

Q **Why does my puppy need company constantly?**
A When you bring your puppy home for the first time, it is unlikely that he will have been isolated at all while in the litter. The contrast between having other puppies around all the time and suddenly finding himself alone is sufficient to cause him a lot of distress, which will set a pattern for future periods of isolation.

Q **Why does he bark and scratch at the door if I leave him alone?**
A The natural response of an isolated puppy is to become distressed and to vocalize in an attempt to get other members of the pack to return and to move around trying to find a way to get to the rest of the pack.

Q **Should I start training him to be alone right away?**
A Since being separated from all that is familiar, being taken to a new home, and meeting a new family can be quite traumatic, give him time to adjust before you begin the process of teaching him to be alone. This will mean that you will need to arrange to be with your puppy constantly if possible for the first few days.

Q **Can I leave him alone at night?**
A To start with, take him into your bedroom at night so that he knows that you are in the same room (this will also help with the house-training process; see page 17).

TIPS FOR SUCCESS

• Be consistent and do a little every day.

• Leave him for a short time at first and gradually work up to longer periods of separation.

• Give him something interesting to chew.

Socializing with people

Being friendly and relaxed with people is an essential quality for a pet dog. Puppies will learn to be sociable if they have plenty of pleasant encounters with many different types of people as they grow up.

It is essential for a pet dog to like people more than anything else in life so that he is friendly toward them, playful, and likes their company. Getting to know people does not happen by accident, and one of the most important things you can do for your puppy is to arrange for him to meet and have fun with different people every day. Doing this will help him to be well adjusted for the world he lives in and will make it much less likely that he will be aggressive to people later in life.

SHY PUPPIES

The process of socialization with people should have been started before you first got your puppy, but unfortunately, many puppies do not receive adequate socialization with strangers while with the breeder.

If your puppy is shy with strangers, you will have to work hard and put in lots of time to catch up. Try to make sure that he has fun with at least one new person every day, working with the same person until he is greeting them happily before moving on to someone else.

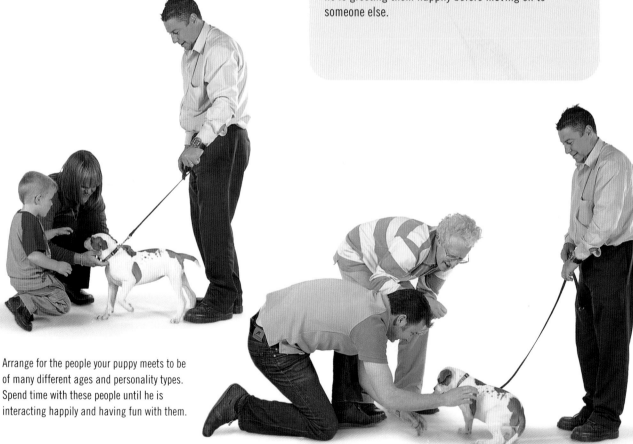

Arrange for the people your puppy meets to be of many different ages and personality types. Spend time with these people until he is interacting happily and having fun with them.

Watch your puppy carefully to see if he is enjoying each encounter and allow him to come forward to meet people in his own time, particularly if he is a little shy at first. Never drag him or force him towards people. Ask visitors not to lean over him and stare if he is becoming anxious, as this puppy is.

Try to find children of all ages, from toddlers to teenagers, who would like to meet your puppy. Give strangers treats to feed him and toys so that they can play with him.

Q&As

Q **My puppy pulls away from people. How can I prevent this?**

A Shy puppies need time to overcome their fears. Ask your visitors to sit or stand quietly and to avoid staring at your puppy. Let your puppy approach them in his own time for treats and games with toys. Make sure that he has plenty of happy encounters every day.

Q **My puppy is overenthusiastic when he meets people. How do I stop him from getting so excited?**

A Control some of your puppy's exuberance by using a lead to keep him from jumping up or on visitors. Give him time to relax and ask visitors to greet him only when he is calm. Make sure that he is well exercised before he meets strangers.

TIPS FOR SUCCESS

• Don't let your puppy pull you toward people. Wait until he is calm before letting him approach.

• Prevent your puppy from jumping up at people by using the lead. Bad habits formed now are difficult to break later on.

• Use food and games with toys to help break the ice with strangers, especially if your puppy is shy. Shy puppies need time to overcome their fears. Ask your visitors to sit or stand quietly and let your puppy come to them.

• Try to find at least two different children for him to meet each week, and more if you can. If you have children in the family, your puppy will need to meet others of different ages and with different personalities.

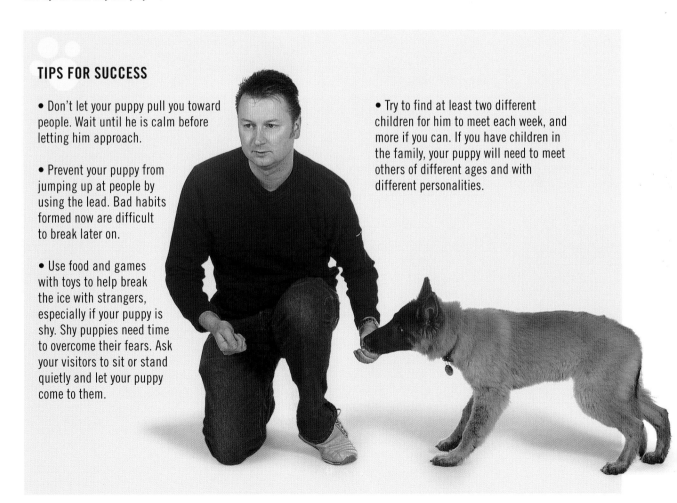

Animals, environments, and noises

As well as people, it is important that your puppy gets used to all the other living and nonliving things he may encounter when he is older. This will help him to see the world as a safe place where he can be happy and relaxed.

Your puppy will need to get used to all the things he will have to encounter in later life. This includes the living part of his environment: people, other dogs, cats, small pets, horses, and livestock; as well as the nonliving part: cars, bikes, noises, different floor surfaces, smells, and environments.

If you don't get him socialized as a puppy, he will grow up being nervous about new experiences. However, if you do it sufficiently, your puppy will grow up to be well adjusted, happy with other animals, and unafraid of new experiences, allowing you to take him anywhere.

Just as with meeting people, this will not happen by accident, and you will need to make an effort to take your puppy out and about as much as possible to many different places and environments. It is important to take things at the puppy's speed and not to overwhelm him with too much at once.

Puppies need to meet other puppies and good-natured dogs so that they can develop their social skills and encounter others without being fearful or rude. Sign him up for a good local training and socialization class, and try to arrange for him to meet and play with other puppies and dogs regularly.

Make sure that any adult dogs he meets are good with puppies before allowing them to get together, as bad experiences are worse than no experiences at all. Stop the play before your puppy is overtired and prevent him from doing anything to other dogs and puppies that you would not like to see him doing when he is older. Equally, protect him from overboisterous play or aggressive dogs if necessary.

NOISES

To prevent puppies from developing noise phobias later in life, get them used to sudden loud noises such as thunder, fireworks, and heavy traffic or trains going past. It is easiest to do this by playing sound-effects CDs, which are readily available from some pet stores and on the Internet. The noises can then be played at a volume your puppy can deal with, allowing him to acclimatize gradually.

Exposure to the real sounds is also necessary, but ensure that they are distant at first and then you can gradually get closer as your puppy learns to deal with the noise.

DIFFERENT ENVIRONMENTS

As well as other animals, it is important to get your puppy used to different environments and to give him plenty of new experiences. Take him into the city, to the country, to the ocean, on buses and trains, to other people's houses, to schools, to pet stores, and to grocery stores. If you take him to all the places where you are allowed to go with him, he will learn to take new experiences in stride. You can then take him anywhere with ease when he gets older.

• Watch for signs that your puppy is feeling pressured by an experience and try to find a way to make him feel more comfortable. This may mean moving farther away from whatever is upsetting him and letting him experience it from a distance for a time before moving closer.

• Don't rush—allow him time to take things in and to realize that he has no need to be afraid.

• Use games with toys and treats to help your puppy overcome any fears.

Provide a safe haven for him to run to by crouching down and calling him to you. Fend off the other dog so that your puppy can feel safe that you are acting as a good pack leader by looking out for him.

Problem solver

If your puppy isn't really interested in you and, consequently, is difficult to train, check to see whether any of the problems listed below apply and follow the suggested solutions. Watch him carefully to find out what makes his tail wag during the day to see what interests him. Try to save whatever interests him for training sessions.

Problem 1
My puppy seems unmotivated.

Some puppies can be difficult to motivate, as they may not be interested in food or games with toys or may show interest for only a short time.
• If you have been using the same toys or treats for a long time and your puppy has lost interest, change to new, exciting toys or tasty treats.
• Think about whether you are using a boring, monotone voice. If so, try giving him praise in a high-pitched, squeaky voice.
• If you are not moving around very much or being exciting—start moving and be more interesting!

Problem 2
My puppy plays more with other dogs than with humans and so is not very interested in people.

• Stop your puppy from playing with other dogs for a while until you get his interest.
• Make sure that he plays with you for three times as long as he plays with other dogs until he is a year old.

Problem 3
My puppy is reluctant to play or train with me.

If your puppy seems unhappy about being trained, think about whether it may be something that you are doing or whether he is just shy.
• If you are very strong-willed and have a sensitive puppy, you need to be gentler and less insistent.
• If a new puppy is too scared to eat or play, allow him longer to settle into your home and learn to trust the people within it.
• If your puppy is reluctant to play in unfamiliar areas, train him in a safe area where he feels secure.
• If you are stressed or tired when training, choose a time for training when you can be more enthusiastic. Puppies will be more willing to work for owners who are happy, eager, and positive.

Problem 4
My usually lively puppy does not seem interested in training.

If your puppy is usually easy to motivate, but does not seem interested in training, it could be because he is anxious about something such as the arrival of a visitor, he is still recovering from an upsetting experience such as a car trip, or he is not feeling well. Think about other common reasons.
• If he has not been to the bathroom, take him to his usual area and encourage him to go.
• If he is full and does not want treats, withhold his food and wait until he is hungry.
• If your puppy has been playing all day, wait until he is ready to play again.
• If he is tired, wait until he is rested. Puppies of giant breeds, in particular, do not have the energy to play for very long before wanting to sleep and should be trained in very short sessions when they wake up and are feeling lively.

ARE YOU READY FOR THE NEXT STAGE?

Does your puppy look at you instantly when you call his name?

Can you hold your puppy's attention for the count of ten?

Does your puppy come running to you when he hears you call, even if he is in another room?

Does your puppy enjoy being handled all over without wriggling?

Will your puppy allow you to dry him all over without biting at the towel?

Does your puppy relax and wait for you to release him rather than struggling when you pick him up, hold him, and hug him?

Does your puppy enjoy meeting people, both adults and children, and go forward to see them willingly?

Does your puppy play nicely with toys and try to avoid putting his teeth on human skin or clothes?

Does your puppy take his face away from the treat if you say "off"?

Will your puppy wait patiently up to the count of ten once you have said "off"?

Sit, stand, down

It is very useful to have a dog who will sit, stand up, and lie down when requested. For example, you can ask your dog to sit if he is muddy and running to greet you, and you may want him to lie down while the vet examines him or stand up while you groom him.

Teaching your puppy to go into sit, stand and down in anticipation of a reward is easy. Teach one position per session to avoid confusion. Lure your puppy into the position using a treat. Put the treat right against his nose and let him chew and lick at it as he follows it. Release the treat as soon as your puppy goes into position and give lots of praise. Once your puppy is readily going into the position, add a voice cue just before your puppy does the required action.

As with human learning, repetition and practice are needed to firmly cement the training in the puppy's mind. Puppies take time to learn new lessons, just as young humans do, so don't expect to train them overnight. You should, however, be making constant, steady progress. If you go wrong and realize you have been rewarding the wrong action, don't worry. Simply adjust your training procedure and reward the behavior you do want in future.

TEACHING YOUR PUPPY "SIT"

1 While your puppy is standing, put the treat against his nose, let him sniff it, and then raise it up slowly over his head. Your puppy should raise his nose and tilt his head back to follow it.

2 Pause here and your puppy will find it easier to put his bottom on the floor than to stand in this position. If he jumps up to get the treat, hold it lower so that he can reach it more easily.

Q&As

Q **My puppy doesn't understand what I want him to do and both of us are getting frustrated. What am I doing wrong?**

A Think about the timing of your rewards. You need to give the treat as soon as your puppy goes into position, not when he has been in that position for a while and is thinking of moving on. Be quick to reward what you want and it will happen more often.

Q **My puppy moves backward instead of sitting. How do I keep him from doing this?**

A Slow your downward hand movement slightly, raise your hand a little so that it goes over his head, or try placing him in a corner so that he cannot move backward.

Q **My puppy lifts his head for the treat when sitting, but gets bored with the treat or with trying. How can I make the process more interesting for him?**

A Change the treats to something more exciting while he learns the exercise. Reward the head lift for a few tries to encourage him, then ask for more.

3 Reward him as soon as his bottom touches the ground.

FOOD LURES, HAND SIGNALS, AND VOICE CUES

The quickest way to get your puppy to learn an exercise is for you to use food as a lure to encourage him to show the correct behavior so that you can reward it. Timing is very important, since the reward needs to be given as soon as the puppy does the right thing. This will link the action with the reward in the puppy's mind and will make it more likely that he will show that behavior again in similar circumstances.

Once the puppy is reliably showing the required action, a hand signal and a voice cue can be added just ahead of the action as a signal to the puppy that a reward is now available for performing that action. Using a hand signal with a voice cue will help him to get the hang of it: voice cues are quite difficult for your puppy to learn, since dogs communicate with body language rather than verbal language. As the puppy begins to understand the voice cues, the signals can be slowly withdrawn (see pages 58–59 on hand signals).

TEACHING YOUR PUPPY "STAND"

1 While your puppy is sitting, put the treat up to his nose, let him sniff it, and then move it slowly away.

2 Keep it just ahead of him so that he cannot reach it, but not so far away that he gives up trying to get it.

3 Stop moving the treat as soon as he begins to get up, then feed him the treat and praise him well as he stands.

Q&As

Q My puppy stays sitting when I move my hand away. What should I do to encourage him to stand up?

A Move your hand more slowly and give him a good reason to get up and follow it with a more appetizing treat.

Q My puppy walks forward instead of just standing up. Am I doing something wrong?

A Stop your hand as soon as you see his back legs unfolding.

TIPS FOR SUCCESS

• Use treats that can be held tightly between your thumb and finger with a bit sticking out for your puppy to lick and chew to keep his attention.

• Move your hand slowly so that your puppy can follow the treat as it moves away from him.

• If your puppy has been trying to get the treat but has been unsuccessful because he is not going into the position, start rewarding small successes, such as lowering or raising his head to encourage him, before asking him to do more.

• Once your puppy is going into these positions easily, practice whenever you have something he wants, such as his dinner, games with toys, or a walk.

TEACHING YOUR PUPPY "DOWN"

1 While your puppy is sitting, put the treat up to his nose.

2 Lure his nose down so that it is between his front legs.

3 Hold the treat there until it becomes more comfortable for your puppy to lie down rather than to sit in this position. Feed him the treat as soon as his elbows touch the floor and give him lots of praise.

Q&As

Q **When I'm trying to get my puppy to lie down, his bottom goes up as his head goes down. How can I cure this?**
A Lure him into the sit position (don't feed him), move the treat down more slowly, and place it close to your puppy's front paws rather than farther away.

Q **My puppy lies down, but gets up again immediately. How can I persuade him to stay down?**
A Give him something comfortable to lie on and train him in a place where he feels secure. Feed another treat quickly after giving the first one so that he remains lying down and is rewarded for it.

4 If you can't get your puppy to lie down, try making a bridge with your legs and lure him underneath it. He will have to lie down to get through.

Coming back on a walk

Teach your puppy to come back when off the lead on a walk from an early age while he is still very interested in being with you. You will need to work harder to be successful than when at home, so use extra-tasty treats and games with toys to help.

Once your puppy is coming reliably to you in the house and garden whenever you call, it is time to practice out on a walk. Even though initially you will be walking him for only short distances to avoid overtiring him or damaging his growing joints and limbs, there should still be plenty of opportunities to practice calling him to you while he is outside in order to get him into good habits for the future.

The younger the puppy, the more he will want to stay close to you for protection rather than wandering off alone, so it is better to let him off the lead sooner rather than later. Puppies under five months will usually be happy to stay close to you, but if your puppy is older, you may want to use a long line at first to give you extra control. (Be careful not to fall over or get tangled in the line and do not use it close to children or elderly people.) Choose a safe, secure area well away from cars, other dogs, and anything that may frighten your puppy. Carry him to and from the area if necessary to avoid walking him too far.

1 Let him explore and run around or wander after you.

2 Call him in the same way as you have been doing at home. Aim for success and call only when your puppy is not investigating anything else and is likely to come to you. As he comes to you, praise him enthusiastically, lure him in to you using the treat, and hold his collar before feeding him. Then let him go again.

Q&As

Q The most convenient place to take him for walks is not fenced off. Is it safe to let him off the lead?

A No. If you can exercise your puppy only in places without secure fences, use a long line to keep him attached to you and try to give him as much freedom as possible.

Q My puppy does not come back when I call, especially in new places. How can I encourage him to do so?

A Try more enticing treats or a game with toys in a less-distracting environment, and be enthusiastic when you call.

SHORT SUCCESSFUL LESSONS

Make sure that lessons last no longer than three minutes. This will help to ensure that neither you nor your puppy gets tired and that you both always leave the session wanting more.

Always finish on a success, if necessary going back to something your puppy already knows so that you can reward him.

Practice every day, with many short sessions throughout the course of the day. Increase the complexity of the exercises gradually and don't be afraid to return to an earlier stage and progress more slowly if your puppy gets confused.

If your puppy doesn't progress as you would like or seems to have forgotten what he once knew, end the session by practicing something easy, then walk away before you get upset and your puppy associates that exercise with your bad reaction. Think of a way to make progress and try something different next time.

3 Aim for about six successful recalls throughout the walk and remember to praise and reward him very enthusiastically each time.

Greeting people without jumping up

Dogs that jump up are a nuisance and can result in ruined clothes, a cleaning bill, and frightened friends avoiding your home. Teaching your puppy not to jump up is easy if you start early, but you must make sure that that you are consistent to ensure long-lasting success.

Puppies jump up to get closer to people's faces so that they can greet and lick them. If this is allowed or rewarded with praise and fuss, it quickly becomes a habit that is very difficult to break later.

In teaching your puppy not to jump up, it is essential that all members of your household make it a rule to greet him only when he has all four feet on the ground. If he learns how to greet the family properly, it will be easier to teach him to be polite with visitors.

1 When visitors arrive, it is best to have your puppy on a lead so that you can control what he does and your visitors do not, unwittingly, teach him bad habits.

2 Let him move forward to greet people only if he has all four feet on the ground. Use the lead to control him if he jumps up. Keep the lead on until you have taught him how to behave well while your visitors are there. You may want to ask some friends to visit for the purposes of training your puppy and learning the handling skills necessary to make this work well. Several sessions will be needed with different people. Continue to use the lead until your puppy can be relied on to treat all visitors politely.

MEETING PEOPLE ON A WALK

Some people do not like dogs and it is important that your dog learns to return to you when you see someone coming toward you. You will then be able to decide whether he should be allowed forward to greet that person or whether he should stay with you. Asking him to come back to you will enable you to put him on a lead, and should the person approaching want to interact with your puppy, you will be able to use it to prevent him from jumping up at the person (remember to reward him well for coming back to you).

Since it is difficult to ask complete strangers to help you train your puppy, crouch down and put a finger in his collar just before he greets them so that you can prevent any jumping up, thereby ensuring that your puppy is rewarded for keeping his feet on the floor.

LEARNING BEGINS AT HOME

When you return home and your puppy is pleased to see you, try to crouch down immediately so that you can put your face close to his to say hello. This removes the need for him to jump up and he can learn what he should do when greeting people.

Hook a finger into his collar so that you can keep him from climbing on you or putting his feet up, and make a big fuss of him.

If you cannot greet him as soon as you walk in the door, it is important that he learns to wait until you are ready and that putting his feet on you will not result in attention.

If he jumps up, turn away slowly without saying anything, ignoring him until the excitement has subsided and he is back on the ground. Then crouch down, praise him well and make a fuss of him.

If your puppy learns how to greet you without jumping up, he will be much more likely to greet visitors in the correct way.

Learning to walk next to you

Before teaching your puppy not to pull on his lead, you need to let him know how rewarding it is to walk next to you. Once he has learned this, it will be much easier to keep his attention.

You need to decide which side you are going to walk your puppy on. You can teach him to walk on either side of you later, but to begin with, choose one side and stick to it (the left side is more common).

ADD VARIETY

Puppies get bored if you offer the same treats all the time. Keep their interest alive by varying the tidbits, keeping their favorite ones for difficult exercises.

Alternatively, use their favorite toy as a reward or lure, and when they perform an exercise well, play a game and have fun with your puppy.

1 Lure him into position with a treat so that he is standing next to your left leg, and reward him well once he is there. Stand still and hold the handle of the lead against your body so that it acts as an anchor in case he chooses to run off.

2 Call his name if you need to get his attention, show him you have another treat, and then hold it up high to prevent him from jumping up while you begin to walk forward.

3 Your puppy should begin to walk with you, concentrating on the treat. After just one or two steps, bend down, feed him the treat, and reward him well, stopping as you do so.

NEXT STEPS

Over several sessions, increase the number of steps you take once your puppy is successfully staying with you, but don't leave it too long before rewarding him in the early stages. Reward him with a treat and plenty of praise when he is walking well beside you.

Once he knows what is required, add a voice cue just before you move off. Repeat, gradually increasing the number of steps you take before rewarding.

Some puppies are not very interested in food and prefer to play with toys instead. If your puppy prefers games to food, use a toy to keep his attention and reward him well for staying with you by throwing the toy for him to play with.

Q&As

Q What can I do to keep my puppy from walking in front of me and tripping me up with the lead?
A Move the reward farther to your side so that he can see it without coming around in front of you.

Q How do I keep him from jumping up at the treat?
A Hold the treat higher so that he sees it is out of reach.

Q What if he does not follow me?
A Encourage him and be very excited and enthusiastic so that he wants to follow you. If he still does not understand, use the treat as a lure for the first few attempts.

Q How do I avoid getting tangled in the lead?
A Whenever your puppy moves out of position, stop and stand still. Use the lead to prevent him from moving away from you, but do not move yourself. Use a treat to lead him back into position—you want him to move to be beside you rather than you moving to be beside him.

Q He keeps losing interest and does not seem to be getting the message. What can I do?
A Stop and rethink what you are doing. Try rewarding him more often when he is in the right place.

TIPS FOR SUCCESS

• Choose a quiet, familiar area in which to practice.

• If your puppy moves away from his place beside your leg, stand still and tempt him back into position.

• Do not twist around if he wraps you in the lead. Let him untangle himself, if necessary by luring him around your body.

• Keep your puppy happy by talking to and praising him whenever he is in position beside you.

Preparation for the vet or groomer

It is important for your puppy to get used to veterinary examinations so that he makes a good patient when he needs to be treated. Teach your puppy to happily accept an examination so that he is not very wriggly, aggressive, or difficult to examine later in life or if he is ill or injured.

Now that he is used to being handled by you, you can prepare him by handling him as a veterinary surgeon would. To do this, you need to teach him to tolerate more intensive handling.

Begin with the gentle handling he is used to so that he relaxes.

Look at and examine every part of him, paying attention to his ears, eyes, teeth, mouth, nails, paws, and under his tail. Make it a pleasant experience for your puppy by giving plenty of praise and by offering occasional treats. Go at a speed he can deal with and be gently persistent so that he learns to accept your attentions and realizes that no harm will come to him.

Practice grooming your puppy using brushes even if he has a short coat that does not require much attention. Hold him by the collar so that he remains still and cannot bite at the brush. Brush slowly along his back at first and continue for just a few minutes on the first day, gradually building up until you can groom him all over. If your puppy has a silky or thick coat, teach him to lie down while you brush him so that you can groom underneath him easily.

If he finds it difficult to accept some things, such as opening his mouth to look at his teeth, go slowly, asking for a small amount of acceptance at first and rewarding well with treats and praise for compliance. Try not to get into a wrestling match with him, as this will be frustrating for you and frightening for him. If he tries to turn his head away when you examine him, hold his head gently and firmly in such a way that he cannot wriggle free. Bring his body in toward you so that he cannot back off or run away. The more secure your hold, the more readily he will accept it. Let him go as soon as he relaxes.

TIPS FOR SUCCESS

• Start very gently and slowly, particularly with a shy, sensitive puppy.

• Hold your puppy firmly and gently so that he cannot pull away.

• Hold him for a very short time at first and gradually increase it.

• Make sure that your fingers are not digging in as you hold him.

• Encourage everyone in the household to do these exercises until your puppy is happy to be handled and examined by everyone in the family.

If your puppy has a coat that will need to be clipped, it is a very good idea to get him used to the noise and feel of clippers running over his body while he is still young. If you don't have clippers, use an electric razor. Remove the blades from the clippers or razor while you practice so that you cannot cut or hurt your puppy accidentally.

GETTING HIM USED TO BEING GRABBED

It is a good idea to get your puppy used to being grabbed, since you or someone else may need to do this one day to save his life. Desensitize him to it gradually by gently grabbing him around the neck and back area. Make sure that you don't use too much force or grab him too hard—you don't want to hurt him. Talk to him and offer a treat or a game afterward so that he associates it with something pleasant and therefore wags his tail and looks for a treat when you do it. Then gradually build it up until you can grab him quickly and firmly when his attention is elsewhere, as you would if he were heading for a busy road.

Food, chew, and bone manners

Some puppies will have already learned to guard food and possessions to keep them safe from other puppies. This can make them protective of food, chews, bones, and toys when arriving in their new household.

If puppies growl, threaten, or bite to keep what they see as theirs, they can get into trouble with humans, and many humans will use punishment to try to solve the problem. Unfortunately, this can lead to an escalation of the puppy's aggression as he tries harder to protect what he wants. Alternatively, the puppy may be intimidated into stopping, but the problem has not really been resolved for them. When they become more confident later in their lives, they may become even more aggressive.

A much better way of dealing with this potential problem is to teach puppies that human hands come to give, not take. If they learn this, they will learn to trust humans and want to have them near their possessions. This stops them from being protective and removes the need for them to be aggressive.

If your puppy is already protective over bones or chews, try the exercise below with his least-favorite chew. Provide him with several chews and allow him to enjoy them until he is nearly tired of chewing before approaching. Practice until he is happy for you to take these low-value chews and then repeat the exercise in later sessions with chews and bones that are progressively more important to him.

1 When your puppy has been chewing his chew or bone for a while, approach him with a very tasty, smelly treat.

2 Show him that you have the treat and use it to lure him away, picking up the chew or bone with the other hand once he is engrossed with trying to get the treat from your fingers.

3 Feed him the treat.

FOOD

While your puppy is eating his dinner, approach him and offer something tastier to eat than his usual food. Offer a second piece, but keep it safe in your hand, putting your hand into his bowl and opening it to reveal the tasty treat. Do this often while he is eating and he will begin to welcome your visits as you bring nicer food than he is eating. Once he begins to welcome you with a wagging tail and steps back from his dish so that you can put something tasty in, occasionally remove his dish, give him a very tasty treat, and then give him his dish back.

TOYS

Some puppies will be protective over toys. If your puppy does this, teach him to retrieve (see pages 118–119) so that he learns to bring things to you rather than you having to go to him to take things away.

In addition, teach him that hands come to give rather than take, so that he learns to trust human hands when they come near his possessions.

TIPS FOR SUCCESS

• To get him used to being touched all over while he eats, start with small strokes and gradually build up. This will make him more tolerant of having people around him while he is eating and he is less likely to react if someone, perhaps a child, unexpectedly touches him or hugs him while he is eating.

• Use very tasty treats: the treat has to be of higher value to him than the chew or food.

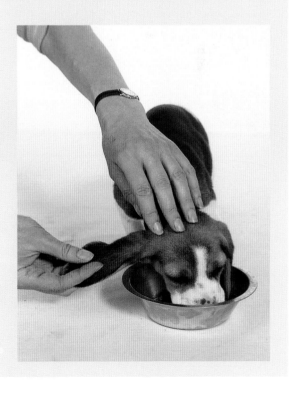

4 Give him back his chew or bone. In this way he will learn that hands coming toward him while he is chewing are giving, not taking, and that there is no need to be possessive over chews or bones.

Problem solver

Since things in the outside world can be very interesting to a new puppy, you may find it difficult to get a good recall at first.

Problem 1

My puppy won't come back to me when out on a walk and now I am frightened about letting him off the lead. He will come reasonably close, but will not let me get ahold of him.

• He may be having too much fun off the lead to want to come back to you. Use a long line so that he can feel as though he is free, with a wide range of movement, even though you are holding the end of it for safety.

• Make sure that he knows you have something that he wants before he goes free, and call him back while he is still quite close to you.

• Run backward, calling excitedly as he moves toward you to increase the excitement, then reward him well for coming.

• Stop trying to reach for him or grab him and let him come to you, sitting down on the ground if necessary so that he knows you will not lunge towards him.

• Use the line to keep him from running off once he is close to you, but don't drag him in with it.

• Be squeaky and silly and make it fun. (It may help to practice this well away from other people.)

• Hold out the treat and draw him in with it until you can reach under his head and take ahold of his collar.

• Change the treats you are using to reward him to something more attractive to him, or try games with toys to see if he prefers them instead. Finding a treat that is more exciting than exploring his new world is essential, but it shouldn't be too difficult to find something that means more once it is combined with your praise and excitement.

• Practice until he is coming quickly every time before removing the line.

• If your puppy is shy, you may have to be gentler when you call and to look away from him, turn sideways, and offer the treat without pressuring him to come forward.

Problem 2
My puppy won't come back if he is playing with other dogs in the park.

• Make sure that he plays with you for longer than he plays with other dogs (about three times longer). He will then associate playing with you as being more exciting than playing with other dogs when he is outside.

• Use a long line to prevent him from running off, and work hard on your recall training. This may mean that you need to start again, encouraging him and practicing until he is reliably coming to you whenever you call. Then repeat when he is near other dogs or things that may be of interest, but use the line to prevent him from getting to them. Call him back and work hard to make sure that you are much more interesting than whatever else he would like to do.

ARE YOU READY FOR THE NEXT STAGE?

Will your puppy readily follow your hand into a sit, a stand, and a down?

Is your puppy happy for you to examine him as a vet does?

Does your puppy stand still when you groom him? Is he happy to have clippers held against his coat and moved over his body?

Is your puppy happy to be grabbed?

Is your puppy happy to let you touch him or put your hand in his food bowl when he is eating?

Does your puppy happily leave his chew or bone when he sees you coming towards him in anticipation of a tasty treat?

Does your puppy come back every time when you call while out on a walk?

Will your puppy walk next to you for fifteen paces when you show him that you have a treat?

Teaching hand signals

Hand signals are a useful bridge between luring and voice cues (see page 43). They are easier for your puppy to learn than words and are especially useful for commands given at a distance or while you are busy talking to someone and need your puppy to respond.

Hand signals are a development of the hand movement that you use when getting your puppy into position using treats (see pages 42–45).

Make a hand signal by adding an exaggerated beginning to the movement needed to lure your puppy into position. Practice without your puppy so that you are good at making an initial hand movement that he will recognize as a command. Flatten your hand to make the signal obvious. When you first begin to teach your puppy, keep a treat tucked under your thumb for

an instant reward when he responds. Your puppy will watch the treat and in so doing watch your hand signal.

After many repetitions, your puppy should begin to respond when he sees the hand signal before you need to lure him into position. When this happens, gradually reduce the movement until it becomes a hand signal only, leaving a gap between the hand signal and lure to give him time to respond. Your puppy will soon learn to go into position as soon as he sees the hand signal so that he gets the treat more quickly.

HAND SIGNALS FOR "SIT"

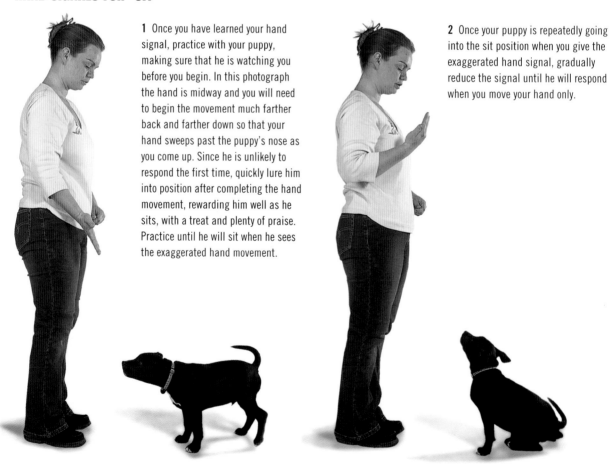

1 Once you have learned your hand signal, practice with your puppy, making sure that he is watching you before you begin. In this photograph the hand is midway and you will need to begin the movement much farther back and farther down so that your hand sweeps past the puppy's nose as you come up. Since he is unlikely to respond the first time, quickly lure him into position after completing the hand movement, rewarding him well as he sits, with a treat and plenty of praise. Practice until he will sit when he sees the exaggerated hand movement.

2 Once your puppy is repeatedly going into the sit position when you give the exaggerated hand signal, gradually reduce the signal until he will respond when you move your hand only.

TRAINING CHECKLIST ✓

Some puppies take quite a while to get the message, so be patient. Continue to make the exaggerated beginning-of-the-hand movement until your puppy responds when he sees it. Gradually reduce the movement until you are just making the hand signal. Remember:

Reward your puppy as soon as you see him beginning to move into position. Do not wait until you have completed your hand movement.

Lure your puppy into position if he doesn't respond to your hand signal after a few seconds. He will then begin to link the hand signal with the action required.

Do not forget to give a voice cue just before you give the hand signal so that he continues to learn to associate the noise you make with his action.

Reward your puppy well with tasty treats and praise—make that tail wag!

JUMPING UP AT THE TABLE

Dogs are natural scavengers and it is normal for puppies to investigate all sources of food. However, puppies need to learn that jumping up at the table is wrong.

• Use the "off" voice cue that you taught him earlier (see page 18) and push him down gently, but do so immediately, before he finds the food. Then show him what he should do instead. Better still, show him what you want him to do before he jumps up so that he never learns to do this.

• Using your hand signal and voice cue for "down," ask him to lie down on his bed.

• Give him a tasty treat or toy as a reward to make it more likely that he will respond next time.

• To prevent him from being interested in the food on the table, give him something interesting to chew.

• He will soon learn that it is more rewarding to stay on his bed. In the early stages of his training, it may be helpful to have his bed close to the table so that you can reposition him easily if he decides to move.

HAND SIGNALS FOR "DOWN"

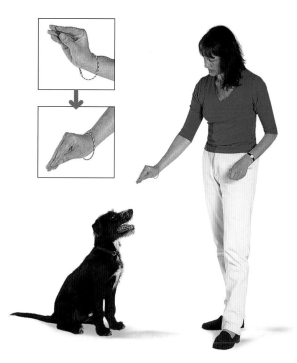

1 Develop a hand signal for "down" by exaggerating the beginning of the movement that lures your puppy into position.

2 Let him watch your hand signal first, then lure him down into position if you need to.

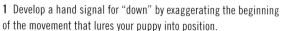

HAND SIGNALS FOR "STAND"

The hand signal for "stand" needs to be done before you lure your puppy into a stand and so it is not as easy as "sit" and "down."

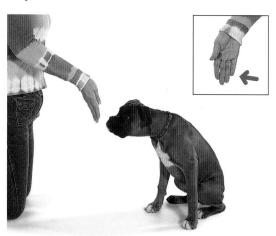

1 Make sure that you have his attention, then give your hand signal as an obvious, exaggerated movement. If he does not respond, lure him into position immediately.

2 Repeat until he begins to anticipate what is needed when he sees the hand signal, then give more time between the hand signal and lure so that he has time to respond.

3 Feed him the treat and praise him well for responding. Repeat many times until he begins to move into position when he sees the hand signal, and then put a gap between the hand signal and lure to give him time to respond.

3 Reward him well when he does the required action.

LEARNING TO SETTLE

It is useful to teach your puppy to "settle," to lie down and rest, so that he will not be a nuisance when you take him to other people's houses or other places where you want him to be still.

Wait until he is tired and you are about to do something quiet such as watch television or read a book. Put him on the lead, sit down, and ask him to "settle" next to your feet.

Use a food lure to get him into the down position and hold the lead so that he cannot move far from you. Ignore him unless he is lying down, then praise him gently and quietly.

Repeat this exercise often at home and then in other people's houses or other places. Once your puppy is familiar with this exercise, repeat when he is excited and active and in different situations so that he learns to settle quickly no matter what is happening around him.

• For an active puppy, give him a chew to keep him occupied.

• Give your puppy something comfortable to lie on.

• If your puppy barks or tries to climb on your lap, put your foot on his lead close to his collar to keep him from climbing up and ignore him until he is quiet and settled. Do not speak or look at him, as this will encourage the unwanted behavior. Praise him gently when he relaxes. Do this exercise often to help him to learn to settle down.

Coming back from something more interesting

It is now time to teach your puppy to come when called, even when he is doing something exciting, so that he will return to you immediately, whatever is happening. This is an important exercise for your puppy to learn, as it could help to keep him from harm.

Until now, you have offered a reward for coming back while he was doing nothing in particular, so there was a real advantage in coming to you. However, when your puppy is doing something more interesting, he may not see the point of leaving to come to you. So it is important to teach him to do so.

Practice the following exercise in many different places such as in the house, yard, and park. When your puppy is responding every time, it is safe to let him off the lead in busier places. Make sure that you are not near traffic when you do so, however, as it is possible that his concentration may lapse initially.

1 Arrange for someone to play with your puppy. When he is really enjoying the game, say his name loudly to get his attention and call him to you.

2 The person playing the game should stop as soon as they hear you say the puppy's name. Wait for him to lose interest in what he was doing.

3 Bring him to you with the treat, praising him as he comes. Hold his collar and feed him the treat.

4 Let him go back to the game he was playing. Repeat this sequence several times a session.

DIFFERENT ASSOCIATIONS

It is important to be aware that when you teach an exercise, your puppy will learn a set of associations surrounding that event rather than just what you are focusing on. If, for example, you always teach your puppy to lie down for his dinner in the kitchen and he begins to lie down in the kitchen when you ask, you may think he knows what the word "down" means. However, you will find that if you take him outside and ask him to lie down, the voice cue will not work.

This is not because he doesn't want to respond, but because he doesn't understand. He needs to be taught the same exercise in many different places and different positions relative to you before he begins to understand that the voice cue, heard anywhere, means that there is a reward on offer for a particular action.

Teach your puppy to sit while he is in any position relative to you, and while you are in different positions too.

• He will begin to understand that "sit" means putting his bottom on the ground whatever he or his owner is doing at the time.

• Practice in a similar way with all the other words that you want him to understand.

TIPS FOR SUCCESS

• Start just a short distance away from your puppy and gradually build up the distance.

• Call excitedly as if you have something really good to offer.

• Make sure that your rewards are worth leaving the game for by using something more tasty than usual.

• Always let your puppy return to what he was doing.

• If your puppy will not leave the person he is playing with, run up to him, show him that you have the treat, and lure him away while running backward before stopping and rewarding him.

• If he prefers a game with a toy to food, use his favorite toy instead of a treat as a reward for leaving the person he is playing with.

Handling by strangers

Now that your puppy is happy to be handled by all members of the family, it is time to get him used to being handled by someone he does not know. This will help him to cope when he has to be examined by veterinary staff, handled by boarding kennel staff, taken to a groomer, or touched by visitors.

Learning to trust people other than those in his family is an important lesson and will help him to be well adjusted and comfortable around others. Wait until he is completely at ease with being handled by all the members of the family before you begin this exercise. If he is not comfortable with family members handling him, go back to the exercises in step 2 (see pages 30–31) and step 3 (see pages 52–53). Once he has learned to trust you, he will find it easier to trust others. Repeat the following exercise as often as possible with lots of different people.

1 Ask someone you know well to handle him as you did during step 2 (see pages 30–31). Ask your visitor to use treats to introduce themselves and lure your puppy to her so that he can be handled.

2 Stay beside him while this happens so that your puppy can feel reassured by your presence. If he wants to come back to you at any time, allow this and ask your visitor to lure the puppy back to her so that he can be handled again. Ask your visitor to stroke him down his back and tail.

3 Ask your visitor to run her hand down each leg, holding each paw as she does so. Ask her to gently stroke the face, head and ears, tail, and under the tummy.

SHY PUPPIES

If your puppy is shy, begin with gentle people whom he tolerates well and gradually work up to people who are more heavy handed or less experienced with puppies.

• Take things very slowly and allow your puppy to build up trust in the person before he or she handles him.

• Go at a speed that your puppy can deal with and don't force him to accept being handled if he is not comfortable with the experience.

• Ask your visitor to play with your puppy every time she or he meets him until he builds his trust in him or her.

• Practice this as often as you can with at least ten visitors so that your puppy learns to trust and enjoy being handled by them.

TIPS FOR SUCCESS

• Explain the procedure to your visitor before he or she begins handling your puppy.

• Ask your visitor to talk to your puppy while he or she handles him.

• Let your puppy come back to you if he wants to.

• Make sure that your puppy is enjoying the experience.

4 If your puppy finds it difficult to accept the visitor touching a certain part of his body, ask her to go slowly, be persistent, and to use treats to help him overcome his fears. Desensitize your puppy to having that part of his body touched over several sessions until he no longer worries or pulls away.

Frustration and attention-seeking

Like children, puppies need to learn that they cannot always have their own way. It doesn't take long and learning this lesson early will result in a much nicer, more compliant dog.

It is important that puppies learn to deal with the feelings that are generated when they cannot have something they want (see page 19). Puppies that do not learn this may grow up barking, nipping, and showing other unwanted behavior when they cannot get their own way. Training him in the way detailed in the steps below will help him to learn to deal with feelings of frustration and he will be more able to handle this in the future.

1 To teach your puppy to deal with frustration, put your puppy on a lead, excite him with something he wants, such as his favorite toy, and throw it just out of reach.

2 Ignore any unwanted behavior and wait until he is calm and relaxed before allowing him to get it. Once your puppy can deal with this, repeat this exercise elsewhere until he can deal with not getting his own way wherever he is.

TIPS FOR SUCCESS

• Start while he is still young and easy to control.

• Begin this lesson in the comfort of your own home rather than in a busy or difficult place such as the vet's waiting room, the car, or a puppy class (just as it is easier to teach children that they cannot always have the sweets they want while at home rather than in a busy supermarket).

• Practice with items that are not so exciting at first and work up to things that your puppy really wants, building up the excitement and anticipation to a high level.

ATTENTION-SEEKING BEHAVIOR

Puppies need to learn that they cannot always be the center of your attention. Outgoing, confident puppies are more likely to try to get your attention by barking, stealing items, or jumping up. If you respond to them, they will rapidly learn that such behavior works.

Worse still, if you ignore low levels of unwanted behavior and wait until your puppy is behaving really badly before responding, the problems can rapidly escalate (particularly if you also ignore good, calm behavior). This will make him very difficult to ignore, especially if you have visitors or you are on the phone.

If puppies learn to get attention in this way, they can be very insistent, especially if you are engrossed in doing something. They will continually watch you for a response while misbehaving, then stop briefly to see if they have been successful before continuing. For some puppies, any attention is better than none, so they will continue even if they are scolded.

• Give your puppy plenty of good-quality attention throughout the day. This is not always easy to do if you have a busy life, but it is important to reward your puppy when he is lying down and being good. So make a fuss of him and play short, exciting games with toys.

• It is important that everyone in the household ignores attention-seeking behavior. Do not touch, speak to, or look at him when he does something designed to get your attention.

• If he has learned to steal things, put all valuable items away and ignore him if he picks up something he shouldn't have. If he has gotten used to getting your attention in this way, his behavior may get worse before it gets better, but, eventually, he will learn that it doesn't get the desired response and will cease to do it.

• Make sure that you reward good behavior as soon as you notice it. This will encourage your puppy to behave well more frequently instead.

Walking on a loose lead

A puppy that walks well on the lead without pulling is much nicer and easier to take for a walk than one that constantly pulls and drags you along. Puppies that walk nicely on leads are more likely to be taken out for walks and will be better exercised and nicer to live with at home.

It is not difficult to teach your puppy not to pull, but you will need to be consistent and persistent and get everyone in the family to work hard with you so that you achieve it while your puppy is still young. Now that your puppy has learned to get rewarded for walking beside you (see pages 50–51), it is time to teach him that pulling against the lead makes you stop moving. Once he learns this, he will try to keep the lead slack so that he can keep walking. This is quite an easy lesson to teach, but you need to be consistent about applying the rule to all lead-walking situations. You must stop and wait **every time** your puppy pulls, and this may mean that you need to allow extra time to get to places if you have a schedule to keep. Eventually, your puppy will try to keep the lead slack so that he can walk without stopping.

1 Choose a quiet place with no distractions to practice in. Keep the lead at a fixed length by holding the handle against your body (make sure that you have a suitable length lead that allows your puppy to travel twice his body length away from you).

2 Stop immediately every time the lead goes tight.

3 Encourage your puppy back to your side.

4 Reward him before moving off again and remember to also reward him well when he keeps the lead slack.

TIPS FOR SUCCESS

• Stop every time the lead goes tight, even if it is not really convenient, such as if you are on a busy street or if you are walking with young children (it is best to train without them at first).

• Give yourself extra time to get to places you need to go so that you can stop and train your puppy without making yourself late (and angry!).

• If your puppy leans into the lead when you stop, vibrate it to get his attention and so that he cannot lean against it, and then lure him back into position.

• Stop and reposition your puppy if he walks in front of you or pulls to the side or behind.

HUMANS ARE SO SLOW

If your puppy was off lead, he would probably walk much more quickly than you. Humans must seem very slow in comparison and it is difficult for young, energetic puppies to curb their enthusiasm for exercise.

• To help them cope, try to walk at a reasonable speed so that your puppy feels he is getting somewhere quickly.

• Energetic puppies find it difficult to walk well on a lead. Before you begin to train them, play energetic games with toys for a few minutes to use up some of their excess energy.

• You may find it easier to train your puppy not to pull when you are on the way home from a walk and he is tired. However, it is worth working hard to train him at the beginning of a walk too, so that he learns how to behave well when he is full of energy.

Boisterousness

Some puppies have a lot more energy than others. Generally, puppies of working breeds are most lively, with the giant and toy breeds being less energetic. If you own a puppy whose ancestors were bred to have lots of energy, enthusiasm, and stamina, you will find that you need to work quite hard to use up all their mental and physical energy.

A well-exercised puppy is a calm puppy. If your puppy is having insufficient exercise, he will have more energy than he knows what to do with and will be hard to live with, hard to train, and constantly doing things that you wish he would not. Since finding an underexercised puppy things to do is hard work, he may often find himself being scolded for doing the wrong thing or being confined for long periods, neither of which is acceptable or good practice. If your puppy is boisterous, constantly energetic, and always getting into mischief, you will need to exercise him more. However, since you cannot walk puppies far because of the risk of damage to their soft bones and joints, you need to use up their energy in other ways.

Try to find a safe place where you can give your puppy freedom to run around off lead. A well-fenced yard that you have easy access to is ideal. This will allow him to burn off his energy and give you a space in which to play games with him.

Energetic games are good for using up energy, especially if you teach your puppy to retrieve so that he is doing all the work instead of you (see pages 118–119). Try to play games that involve lots of activity for your puppy and need only a small amount of effort from you. For example, teach your puppy to find a hidden toy (see pages 120–121) and then hide toys out of sight for him to find.

AN EXERCISED PUPPY IS A CALM PUPPY

If you have a boisterous, lively puppy, try to exercise him well before you want him to be calm, such as before visitors arrive, before traveling in the car, and before a training session. In this way, you can reward good behavior without having to prevent or stop behavior that is unwanted.

SHORT SESSIONS WITH YOUR PUPPY

It is important not to play so much that your puppy is exhausted, as this will put strain on his body and may cause injuries. Have frequent short sessions of play throughout the day so that he has plenty of time to rest and recover in between play sessions. Once you have taken the edge off his physical energy, training sessions will help to use up mental energy.

OLDER DOGS ARE MORE ENERGETIC

As your puppy gets older, he will develop more energy and stamina. Be prepared for this and provide more things for him to do, more things to explore, and more outings to go on to use up his energy as he grows.

NEED A PUPPY-SITTER?

If you have a puppy with lots of energy and you work long hours, he will probably need more exercise and entertainment than you can provide. Find someone who is willing to puppy-sit and come into your home to break up your puppy's long hours alone with games and fun.

Finding someone who would like to look after your puppy during your working hours would be an even better solution.

TIPS FOR SUCCESS

• Exercise your puppy well to use up excess energy before trying to get him to concentrate on training.

• Match your puppy's play and training program with his requirement for exercise so that he is calm and content.

• Mental exercise can be more tiring than physical exercise, so try to get the balance just right by planning activities for your puppy's brain and body.

• Providing your puppy with plenty of things to chew and explore (see pages 20–21) will keep his interest and use up some of his mental energy.

Problem solver

Educating a young puppy takes time, thought and patience. Time spent on solving problems now will help to prevent problems from becoming stubborn bad habits later.

Problem 1
My puppy digs up the yard.

Digging up plants in the yard is a favorite puppy pastime if they are left alone outside for too long. This natural behavior can be very destructive and also annoying for the owners, especially if they take pride in their yard.

• Supervise your puppy when he is outside and teach him what you want him to do there instead.

• Give him things to chew and play games with him. Then bring him inside to relax.

• If you want to leave your puppy outside for short periods of time, watch him through the window or make sure that he is in a special fenced-off area where he cannot do any damage. Supervise at first to ensure that he feels safe there and is not worried, and don't leave him there for too long or he will begin to display other unwanted behavior, such as barking.

Problem 2
My puppy starts barking when I produce the lead and won't stop.

Puppies often bark with excitement and this can quickly become a habit. Your puppy needs to learn that barking results in you stopping all preparations for the walk.

• Whenever he barks, stop and keep still, look away and don't speak, and wait until you can count up to three in silence before continuing. Repeat this immediately whenever he barks.

• Allow a lot of time at first for walks, be patient, and you will find that he quickly realizes that barking makes you stop rather than speed up.

Problem 3

My puppy barks when I am on the phone.

A puppy that is used to getting his own way may find it difficult to accept being ignored while you pay attention to your caller. Since it is difficult to speak on the phone while a puppy is barking, this behavior is often unwittingly rewarded with attention in an attempt to stop the noise.

• Teach your puppy to accept being ignored at other times.

• Pretend to talk to someone on the phone. Then, later on, arrange to have someone call you so that you can practice ignoring your puppy when he barks. Reward him when he stops by stroking him gently.

ARE YOU READY FOR
THE NEXT STAGE?

Does your puppy respond to your hand signal for "sit" and go into position at once?

Does your puppy respond to your hand signal for "stand" and go into position at once?

Does your puppy respond to your hand signal for "down" and go into position at once?

Will your puppy settle down easily when you are at home and at friends' houses, even when he is excited?

Does your puppy come back to you when you call, even when he is very interested in something else?

Is your puppy happy to have different people handle him all over?

Does your puppy adjust the speed at which he walks when on a lead so that the lead stays loose?

Coming when called—introducing random rewards

One of the biggest objections to using rewards for training is that you always have to have pockets bulging full of treats and toys. However, it is necessary to reward continuously only when your puppy is learning.

Once your puppy has learned what a voice cue or hand signal means, it is better if his responses are rewarded intermittently (for example, two times out of ten) rather than all the time. Make sure that your puppy has learned the exercise well and is responding every time before reducing the rewards. Otherwise, he will get very confused. It is also very important to continue to praise your puppy every time he has responded well.

1 Now that your puppy has learned to come back when called, even when he is doing something else, it is time to begin reducing the rewards he receives.

2 Call him to you and be as pleased with him as you were when he first came, but reward one response in every three with games or treats. Gradually extend this until you are rewarding once only in every five times at random.

GRADUAL TRANSITION

It should be a gradual transition between rewarding constantly and variably. For example, start by rewarding eight times out of ten at first, then six, then five, and so on. Random rewards can be a very difficult concept to put into practice, as you will be used to rewarding him constantly and may feel mean about not doing so. However, if you can do this, there are great benefits, as your puppy cannot anticipate when he will get the reward and so he will work longer and harder for the same amount of reward than if he was rewarded continuously.

JACKPOTS

To make training even more fun for your puppy and to make it even more likely that he will respond, offer occasional jackpots. These are a special treat, an abundance of treats, or several really nice things at once. Jackpots need to be extra special, so have fun, dance around, and celebrate with your puppy! It is like winning the lottery, and the dog will begin to gamble on the outcome and continue to respond just in case the jackpot comes through. If you save jackpots and rewards for when your puppy responds particularly well, then his performance will improve.

Q&As

Q **I am finding it difficult not to give rewards every time or at random. Is there any way I can make it easier for myself?**

A Put ten buttons in your pocket, two of which are colored. Mix them up and pull out a button before you call your puppy. If it is one of the colored buttons, reward your puppy with a treat; if it isn't, then don't. If your puppy can predict when he will get a reward and stops responding when he thinks he will not, you need to be more random with your rewards. Keep him guessing when the treat will appear.

Q **Why does reducing the rewards lead to an improvement in response?**

A It may seem strange, but scientific experiments have shown that animals will work harder if they are rewarded occasionally at random rather than constantly. The animal is happy to make the effort needed to gamble on the outcome, becoming excited at the idea of a possible win. The principle works for humans too and is the idea on which national lotteries and slot machines are founded. It can be used very effectively to improve the response of your pet in training.

TIPS FOR SUCCESS

• Save the treats for good responses.

• Save jackpots for exceptional responses.

• Always praise your puppy when he has responded correctly to let him know that he has done the right thing, even if you do not give him a treat.

• Always give a treat if your puppy comes back to you from something he is interested in or has had to run a long way to get to you.

Positions, different places, and random rewards

Now that you have taught your puppy to respond to hand signals, it is time to reinforce his understanding of these signals by teaching him to respond in different places, where there are more exciting distractions.

Practice hand signals when your puppy is in different positions relative to you. For example, ask him to respond when you are sitting in an armchair, standing in front of him, or standing beside him. In this way, he will begin to generalize so that he will act on your hand signals wherever he is in relation to you. If he doesn't respond, give him a few moments to think about what he needs to do and then use a food lure

to get him into position. Remember to praise him well and give a treat when he does the right thing.

Remember also to continue to give the voice cue just before the hand signal so that your puppy learns the association between voice cue, hand signal, and the action required. This will make it a lot easier to teach him to respond to the voice cue only later in your training (see pages 90–91).

1 Teach him anywhere, whenever you think of it, for example, when out in the park, in the yard, or at a friend's house. It takes only a few seconds to give the hand signal and reward him for responding. By doing this, you will be building up his knowledge of what he has to do so that he will respond wherever he is.

2 Ask him to respond whenever it will be useful to you, for example when he needs to stand up so that you can dry him underneath with a towel if he is wet from a walk or bath.

TIPS FOR SUCCESS

• Get your puppy's attention and give a hand signal in busy places when he is least expecting it. Reward well for a response.

• Begin to give your puppy random rewards in places where he is familiar with being rewarded for a response. He will learn that sometimes he will get rewarded there and may even get a jackpot.

• Always praise your puppy for complying with requests, even if he is not getting a treat or game for that response.

• Remember to have fun and celebrate with your puppy when you give a jackpot.

VARIABLE REINFORCEMENT

Once your puppy is reliably responding to hand signals in any location, wherever you are in relation to him and whatever is going on around you, it is time to reduce the amount of rewards he is given.

Reduce your rewards slowly until you are giving treats for two in every ten responses at random (see page 74). Save the treats for the best performances, but praise every time your puppy responds so that he knows he has done the correct thing.

Remember to give occasional jackpots for any exceptional performances, such as lying down when another dog runs past.

3 Once your puppy is responding to hand signals in lots of different places, begin to teach him to respond when there are other things going on around him. Start with distractions that are not too exciting like people walking past in the distance. Then gradually work toward something that your puppy may prefer to do instead of what you are asking.

4 Remember to reward him well when he does something new for the first time. Once he knows what is required, use variable reinforcement to achieve a better response.

Greeting strangers in a sit

Not everyone likes dogs, and some people are scared of them. For this reason, it is important that your puppy greets guests and strangers by sitting and waiting until they approach him rather than by running toward them and jumping up.

If you have been teaching your puppy to greet strangers by not jumping up (see pages 48–49), you will have laid the foundation for this exercise and will have made it easier for your puppy to learn.

The easiest way to teach this exercise is to ask a few friends to help you. Find a house or another suitably sized building that you can walk around, and ask your helpers to slowly walk one way around a building while you walk around in the other direction with your puppy until you meet.

If possible, try to arrange several of these sessions, even if you have to use family members instead of visitors. Then try to arrange encounters with friends in the park or on walks so that you can practice this exercise. Teach your puppy the same lesson until he is reliably sitting when he approaches new people.

1 When you meet someone, ask your puppy to sit. Ask the person to come forward to greet your puppy only when he is sitting and to back away if he stands up.

2 If he gets up, they should slowly turn away. Ask him to sit again, luring him into position if necessary so the person can come forward again.

3 After a few repetitions with different people, you will find that your puppy learns that the way to get people to move closer is to sit still and let them come to him. Continue until he automatically sits to greet people as they approach.

FRONT-DOOR ETIQUETTE

As well as practicing outside, you will also need to practice in the house, particularly at the front door. Try to find a number of friends who would be prepared to run through this exercise with you until your puppy will sit easily and stay sitting while visitors come in to greet him.

Continue with this exercise, asking them to repeat this procedure, until your puppy sits and remains sitting without any prompting from you as you open the door to allow the visitor to come in.

Q&As

Q **My puppy is lively and excitable and I am finding it very difficult to keep him still. What shall I do?**

A Ensure that your puppy has had plenty of exercise, so that he is tired enough to remain calm, before you try to teach this exercise.

Q **My partner insists on allowing our puppy to jump up at him when he arrives home. Will it be possible to train him not to jump up at visitors?**

A Yes, but it will be more difficult if he is occasionally rewarded for doing the wrong thing, particularly as this behavior is so rewarding in itself. Try to get your partner involved in the training so that he can appreciate how difficult it can be and perhaps he will be less likely to allow your puppy to learn the wrong thing in future.

Q **My puppy sits but then jumps up again as soon as visitors crouch down to pet him. How can I keep him in the sit position?**

A Ask the visitors to withdraw as soon as they see him begin to move out of position. Keep repositioning him and ask them to move toward him very slowly when they reach down to reward him so that they are not inducing more excitement that will encourage him to get up.

TIPS FOR SUCCESS

• Make sure that everyone in the family greets your puppy when he is sitting. If he has good habits with his favorite people, it will make it easier for him to greet visitors well.

• If your puppy is finding it hard to stay in the sitting position, make sure that he has had a lot of exercise beforehand so that he is tired and more likely to wait until people come to him instead.

• If your puppy is very sociable and is finding it difficult to stay sitting as people approach, ask everyone to slow their movements down so that your puppy is less excited.

Getting used to veterinary examinations by strangers

Now that your puppy is comfortable about being handled by strangers and about you examining him as a veterinary surgeon or groomer would, it is time to get him used to strangers doing this to him too.

Many puppies are not handled and restrained enough by people other than their owners and, as a result, can become anxious when they need to go to the groomer's or be examined by the vet. If your puppy is unhappy about being touched and restrained by people whom he does not know, he may try nipping, growling, or other forms of aggression to get himself released. This can result in people being rough with him to get compliance or a less-thorough examination by the vet if he or she cannot examine him easily.

Before you do these exercises, make sure that you can handle your puppy all over and examine him as a vet would without him wriggling or objecting in any way (see pages 52–53). Also make sure that strangers can do the same before they begin this exercise.

If, during the following exercise, there is something that your puppy particularly does not like, ask your helper to skip that part and make sure that you work on desensitizing your puppy to it before asking someone to do it again another day.

1 Ask your helper to lead your puppy a short distance away and spend a few moments getting to know him so that he feels comfortable with her.

2 Ask her to gently look in his ears and eyes.

3 Then get her to examine each of his paws. Ask her to pick up your puppy, hold him, and restrain him, letting him go when he is calm.

VARYING THE LOCATION
Try to get several people to do these exercises in different locations until your puppy is very accepting of being handled and examined in this way wherever he is. Different puppies will take varying amounts of time to accept being handled by other people, so continue with these exercises for as long as it takes for your puppy to become comfortable with other people handling him in this way.

Q&As

Q My puppy gets worried or panics when taken away from me. How can I get him used to it?

A Go more slowly and decrease the distance that he is moved away from you. Ask your visitors to play a game with him, feed him treats, and talk to him gently to gain his trust before moving him farther away.

Q My puppy struggles when people begin to examine him and tries to get away. How can I overcome this?

A Work harder at getting him to accept gentle handling from strangers before working on getting him used to being examined. Make sure that he is happy about you handling him and examining him before asking others to do so.

4 Get them to look underneath his tail.

5 Since this is a training exercise, take care to deal with anything he objects to by asking your helper to go more slowly in that area and asking her to offer treats for compliance. Ask her to be gently persistent, but not to rush your puppy into accepting.

Getting used to all types of humans

Your puppy needs to get used to all sorts of people if he is to grow up well adjusted and unafraid. If your puppy is content to be around anyone, then you can relax in the knowledge that he will be happy wherever you go.

Try to get him out to meet a wide variety of people. If this is not possible, the next best thing is to get him used to unusual attire by getting family or friends to dress up in different items. If you find that your puppy is worried by a particular appearance, try to expose him to it in small doses every day until he gets used to it.

Use games and treats to increase his acceptance of anything unusual. For example, introduce him to people using walking sticks or crutches, wearing sunglasses, dark clothes, beards, hats, or motorcycle helmets, or carrying umbrellas, bags, or backpacks, as well as to people on bikes or in wheelchairs, children in strollers, and people who come from different ethnic backgrounds.

Meeting someone wearing a motorcycle helmet will help this puppy to realize that people with odd appearances are friendly, not frightening.

Hats can change our appearance and make some shy puppies scared. Walking with a limp or using a walking stick can also make us appear very different from the puppy's perspective.

Imagine meeting this on the doorstep during Halloween! Puppies need to get used to this type of thing early in life if they are to cope later.

Umbrellas can be scarce in summer, so puppies need to get used to them opening, closing, and twirling around in preparation for winter.

TIPS FOR SUCCESS

• Take care not to scare your puppy when he first sees you or anyone else with a new appearance—scary first impressions can last a lifetime.

• If your puppy is looking worried, lead him away, make a fuss of him, play a quick game, or feed him a few treats to lighten the mood, and then try again.

• Ask the stranger or person who has dressed up to offer games with toys or treats to speed up your puppy's acceptance.

• Try to think of all the unusual things that people do or wear and make sure that your puppy accepts all of these happily before he matures.

Traffic and walking with turns

Now that your puppy has learned to keep the lead loose and has learned how rewarding it is to walk next to you, you can take this a stage further.

Find a quiet place with no distractions and practice making turns and walking around objects. Set up a few objects to walk around or use natural obstacles. Figure out where you are going before you begin to walk so that you can concentrate on teaching your puppy to turn with you. Before you change direction, warn him by saying his name and encouraging him to walk next to you. Slow down and keep him at your side, and be sure to encourage him and praise him when he is in the correct position.

When your puppy can do these exercises easily, keep things interesting by speeding up to a run, then slowing down for a few paces. Keep your puppy guessing what you will do next so that he concentrates on you. When he is looking at you, make sudden turns and changes in direction, encouraging him to move with you and rewarding him well when he does. By doing this, your puppy will learn to think about you and where you will be going when he is on the lead rather than thinking about where he wants to go instead.

WALKING NEAR TRAFFIC

Put yourself between the car and your puppy. This can help to give him a feeling of security. Also, while he is very young, try to walk him on quiet roads or roads with wide sidewalks so that he does not have to get too close to fast-moving traffic until he is used to it.

Teach your puppy to sit beside you at the curb before you cross the road. He will then be under control and less likely to pull you into the traffic. If you have taught him to sit beside you elsewhere, he should be happy to do so at the curb, but if he hesitates, lure him into position using a treat and then reward him well for sitting.

TIPS FOR SUCCESS

• Let your puppy know that you are about to turn or change course by getting his attention and asking him to walk closer to your leg.

• Remember to stop **every time** the lead goes tight when you are in more distracting situations so that your puppy learns to pay attention to keeping the lead loose at all times.

• Keep yourself between your puppy and the traffic so that he feels protected and can concentrate on walking well on the lead.

Always keep your puppy on a lead when on a road, even if you think he is well trained. He could see a cat or something even more exciting and momentarily forget about your requests for him to walk beside you.

SCARED OF TRAFFIC

If your puppy is very scared of traffic or tries to chase cars and buses, you will need to take things more slowly to help him overcome his fear. If this is not done early, he may always be afraid of traffic or may become obsessive about chasing cars and other vehicles.

• Take your puppy to a place where you can put plenty of distance between him and a busy road so that he feels relaxed enough to play and eat.

• At this distance, play games with him and offer tasty treats so that he begins to get good associations with vehicles. Be happy and make it as much fun as you can.

• Continue in this way, getting slowly closer to the traffic while playing and offering treats.

• Repeat these sessions, gradually getting a little closer each time, until your puppy is happy to walk down the sidewalk next to the traffic. For some sensitive puppies, this can take many weeks. However, going slowly in this way and never forcing your puppy to get closer than he feels comfortable with will ensure lasting success.

Wait/stay

"Wait" or "stay" is a useful command for your puppy to learn, as there will be lots of times when you want him to stay still for a moment while you do something else. This is an easy exercise to teach if you make sure that he is well exercised first.

The "wait" command can be useful in a variety of situations where you want your puppy to stay still until he is given further instructions. Although keeping still is difficult for young puppies, teaching them to keep themselves in the same place until you reward them is possible. It is easier if you practice in short, successful sessions.

Practice the following exercise a few times and then gradually build up the time your puppy waits.

End the first session when your puppy can stay still for a count of five, then practice over many sessions, gradually building up the time your puppy can wait.

Once your puppy understands that he is just required to sit and wait, practice this exercise many times a day in different places in the house, garden and outside. Ask him to sit and wait before doing something he wants to do, such as going through a doorway or before being given his dinner.

1 Lure your puppy into a sit position beside you.

2 Get his attention by saying his name and, if necessary, showing him that you have a treat.

3 Ask him to wait and give a hand signal. Count to two and reward him well while he remains in position. If he tries to move, use the lead to prevent him from moving too far and lure him back into position with a treat (don't feed the treat—wait until he has kept still before doing so).

"STAY" OR "WAIT"?

The word you use to ask your puppy to wait is not important, but it is essential to use just one word. So choose a word, such as "wait" or "stay," and use that word only.

Some people differentiate between "wait" and "stay" by using "wait" for times when you will call your puppy away from that position (e.g., if you have asked him to wait while you walk through a door ahead of him) and using "stay" for times when you will go back to him, as in an obedience test. However, the puppy still has to learn to stay still until given another signal, so it is not really necessary to differentiate between the two voice cues until you get to higher levels of training.

4 Reward him well while he is still in position, as you will then be helping him to realize what he is being rewarded for. Give him treats and praise him gently so that he does not get excited and get up. Stop rewarding if he moves out of position.

Q&As

Q My puppy has too much energy and won't listen. Am I doing something wrong?

A The wait is an easy exercise to teach if your puppy is well exercised. If you wait until your puppy has had plenty of exercise, play, and training, he will not mind keeping still. Trying to teach this exercise to a puppy that is full of energy is much more difficult.

Q Should I get him to sit or lie down?

A You can teach your puppy to wait in either position. Choose one position and keep to it until your puppy understands what he is supposed to do before teaching him to wait in a different position. The wait in a sit is more useful as your puppy is likely to be asked to sit and wait more often than to lie down and wait.

Q Should I use a hand signal or voice cue?

A As for all exercises, hand signals are learned more quickly than voice cues, so giving your puppy a clear hand signal will help to teach him what is required more quickly. When teaching the puppy to wait, both signals can be taught at the same time, with the voice cue being given just ahead of the hand signal.

Q Where should I get my puppy to wait?

A It does not matter if you teach your puppy to sit beside you or in front of you, although it is slightly easier to correct any movement if he is sitting beside you.

Q My puppy waits at the door when I ask him to but then quickly tries to get through the door. How do I keep him still?

A Reward him when he is in the wait position more often rather than rewarding him by calling him through the door. He will then begin to anticipate the reward for staying still rather than anticipating that you will call him through the door.

Problem solver

Problems can arise if your puppy is undersocialized and is shy, as well as if he is well socialized and very enthusiastic about meeting people. Teaching him how to behave well with other people while he is still young and small is important.

Problem 1

My puppy is worried about strangers and backs away when they try to touch him.

• Make sure that people in the family can handle him all over without resistance before inviting strangers to do this.

• It is important to let him approach people in his own time. Do not force him to accept being touched or he will never learn to enjoy the experience and may learn to become aggressive to protect himself.

• Try to arrange for someone he likes to visit every day for a while. Give them tasty treats and toys to give him to help encourage him to move toward them, but let him retreat if he wants to.

• Ask them not to stare at him and to talk to him softly. Sometimes the intensity of meetings like this are too much and it may help to take him out for a short walk with the person first so that he is already familiar with them by the time they come back into the house. Once he begins to trust them, they can try running

their hand down his back in return for a treat. Continue until your puppy is happy to be handled by this person and then move on to someone else, continuing in this way until he is confident with all strangers.

Problem 2

My puppy jumps up at my children when they come home from school and jumps up at their friends when we meet them in the park.

• You will need to control your puppy when he meets all children so that you can teach him the correct way to greet them.

• When at home, try putting him in his playpen or use stair gates to separate him from the children until they have come in and the excitement has died down.

ARE YOU READY FOR THE NEXT STAGE?

Is your puppy now working hard at coming back when called to try to win a jackpot?

Is your puppy working harder at getting into the right position when you give a hand signal to try to win a jackpot?

Does your puppy sit automatically when greeting visitors either outside or at your home?

Does your puppy sit or stand to greet members of the family when they arrive home without jumping up?

Is your puppy happy to have people he does not know take him away from you and handle him all over?

Is your puppy comfortable with a wide variety of human appearances?

Does your puppy walk with you when you turn corners and go around obstacles?

Is your puppy happy to walk with you when you are near traffic?

Can your puppy stay sitting when you ask him to wait while you count to five or more?

• Teach your children to stand still, fold their arms, and slowly turn their face away from your puppy when he jumps. When all of his four feet are on the ground, they should bend down to greet him, diverting him from further jumping by encouraging him to play with a toy instead.

• Teach your children and their friends how to greet him properly and supervise them constantly to ensure that the puppy learns correctly.

• Use his lead and collar to stop him from jumping on children that he meets in the park and ask them to wait until all four of his feet are on the floor before they greet him.

Sit, stand, down—learning to respond to voice cues only

Although spoken words are more difficult for your puppy to understand than hand signals, they are a lot easier for us to use. You have been using the words throughout the training, so teaching your puppy to respond to the voice cue only should be quite easy.

Throughout training, you will have given the voice cue just before lures and hand signals, and therefore your puppy will already be associating the sound with the action required. Teaching your puppy to respond to voice cues only is useful for times when you want a quick response and are not free to give hand signals. Remember that it is relatively difficult for dogs to learn to respond to spoken words, so teach this exercise patiently until your puppy understands what is required. Once your puppy understands the voice cues, first practice in different places, and then practice with distractions going on around you. Finally, reduce the rewards given and add jackpots.

1 To teach your puppy to respond to voice cues only, make sure that you have his full attention, give the voice cue, and then wait a few seconds before giving the hand signal. Repeat until your puppy begins to go into position when he hears the voice cue only.

2 Praise enthusiastically as soon as he begins to go into position, and give the treat when he completes the action. Since your puppy is learning something new, reward enthusiastically every time he gets it right. Teach the voice cue for one position only during each session to avoid confusing your puppy.

IF HE DOES NOT UNDERSTAND

If he hesitates for longer than two seconds and doesn't seem to understand, help him out with a hand signal or food lure. Keep practicing all positions until your puppy will respond to any voice cue wherever he is. Usually, pet dogs learn to respond only to "sit," as owners repeat this often in many places. Once your puppy is responding to the voice cue every time, practice in different places and in real-life situations. To ensure that your puppy learns to respond to "down" and "stand" too, repeat and reinforce these commands in lots of different environments and circumstances.

POSITIONS AT A DISTANCE

Once your puppy understands voice cues and responds readily when he is standing near to you, you can begin to teach him to respond at a distance.

Since your puppy has been rewarded for sitting, standing, or lying down near to you, his natural reaction if you ask him to respond at a distance is to get close to you first. For this reason, you need someone to hold him a short distance away while you ask him to respond.

• Give him time to figure out what is required and wait until he has responded. If he does not respond, ask him again, and this time, run forward and lure him into position, rewarding him well when he does the required action.

• Repeat until he takes up the position required when you are a short distance away. Praise and reward him well when he responds. (Since he is learning something new, go back to rewarding him every time he gets it right.)

• Continue until he responds without struggling to get to you and then gradually increase the distance. Eventually, you can do this without the person holding him, but always go to him when giving him his treat/toy so that he is rewarded for sitting, standing or lying down where he is rather than beside you.

TIPS FOR SUCCESS

• Say the voice cue clearly.

• To help your puppy understand, say each voice cue with a slightly different inflection.

• Make sure that you do not say "sit down" instead of "sit," as this will easily be confused with "down."

Coming back from distractions when called

Now that your puppy has learned to come back when you call, even when he is having fun playing (see pages 62–63), it is time to teach him to come back during enjoyable real-life events, such as when he is eating his dinner, running up to someone, or playing with other dogs.

Most owners never teach this exercise and wonder why their puppy will not come back to them when he is doing something more exciting. Don't expect him to come when called just because he knows the word. He needs to be taught that it will be worth his while to come when called whatever he is doing.

Make a list of all the situations where you may need to call your puppy away when he is doing

something that he enjoys. Then practice with each one of these situations in turn until your puppy will come back to you right away whenever you call.

It is difficult for your puppy to leave something he is enjoying, so you will have to make sure that he knows it will be worth his while to respond well. You can do this by letting him know that you have something really good to reward him with when he does so.

1 Let your puppy play for a while with the other dog, then ask the owner to hold the dog while you call. Ask him to fend off your puppy so that it cannot play with the other dog.

2 If your puppy does not respond to your first call, lure him away from the other treat, running backward and making it fun for your puppy to come with you before rewarding.

PUNISHMENT

Never punish your dog for not coming back to you immediately, no matter how long he took, whatever he did until he came, and however angry you are. If he came back to you, he needs to be rewarded so that he repeats the behavior next time. If he is slow, consider it to be a failure of your training strategy and think about how you can teach him more successfully.

PRACTICE MAKES PERFECT

Practice calling him away from things he may like to chase, such as people on bikes and children who are running. Set up situations where you can ask the riders or children to stop as soon as you call, and play an exciting chase game with a toy when your puppy gets to you.

TIPS FOR SUCCESS

• If you think there is a chance that your puppy may not respond, increase the chances by getting closer or calling more loudly and urgently.

• Practice calling your puppy back a few times on each walk, not just when you want to put him on the lead to go home. Give plenty of praise when he comes to you, as well as occasional rewards and a few jackpots.

• Don't get boring now that he is coming to you regularly; try to remember how happy you were when he came to you the first time and be just as enthusiastic each time he returns.

3 Reward him well for coming to you, holding his collar for a few moments while you have fun with him.

4 Then let him free to play again. Practice until he will come to you readily when he is playing with other dogs or puppies before letting him free with dogs in an open area.

Getting used to being handled on a table

Unless you regularly groom your puppy on a table, being placed on a surface up high may not be something he is familiar with. To make sure that he is happy with this, particularly when he has to be examined by the vet, it is a good idea to practice this at home until he feels comfortable and secure.

To get your puppy ready for being examined at the vet, you will need to teach your puppy to accept being placed on a table and to be comfortable with being handled and examined there. If your puppy is worried about being on the table, put him on it several times a day and feed him his favorite treats or his dinner there. Continue until he begins to enjoy being there, and then get him used to being handled and examined.

1 Lift him on to the table slowly and gently to give him time to get used to being up high.

2 Make sure that he cannot fall off by holding on to him all the time. Begin slowly, giving your puppy time to accept being on the table.

3 Practice until you can quickly and efficiently look at his ears, eyes, teeth, mouth, paws, and under his tail.

GETTING OTHERS TO EXAMINE HIM ON THE TABLE

Once your puppy is comfortable with you examining him on the table, ask a friend to help your puppy to get used to other people handling him as a veterinary surgeon or groomer would. Ask them to lift him on to a table and look at his eyes, ears, teeth, mouth, paws and under his tail.

Ask them to brush him and to use a towel to pretend to dry him. Ask them to go at the puppy's speed so that they don't overwhelm him with too much at first.

Supervise from a distance and help your puppy out if he is getting worried. Ask them to make it fun for your puppy and to give occasional treats.

DEALING WITH A SHY PUPPY

Take things more slowly. Start by getting him to accept treats from visitors when he is on the table while you stand beside him. Once he is happy with this, get him used to the visitor stroking him and gradually work up to having them handle him as he builds his trust of them. Ask the visitor to stop before you think your puppy will have had enough and repeat again the next day until he is comfortable.

Practice as often as you can with at least ten different people so that your puppy gradually learns to trust people and enjoy the experience.

TIPS FOR SUCCESS

• Reward him well for keeping still while you examine him.

• If the table surface is slippery, place him on a nonslip pad, such as a bath mat.

• Begin with gentle people who will take things more slowly.

• Work up to people who are used to handling dogs and will be more efficient in their handling.

NAIL CLIPPING

Practice pretending to clip your puppy's nails regularly so that he is happy to have it done when it needs to be done for real. You should not clip your puppy's nails until you have been shown how to do it properly by a qualified person, but you can get him used to the actions.

Sit down on the floor with him and tuck his body against yours so that he feels secure and he cannot wriggle away. Hold one of his paws gently but firmly, spread out his toes gently and put the nail clippers against his nail. Reward him with a small treat for keeping still and go more slowly if he will not.

Begin with just one nail at first and then work up until you can pretend to trim all his nails easily. Continue with each paw until he remains calm and then reward him.

Barking

Barking is more common in the smaller breeds, especially terriers, who are easily aroused. It can become a nuisance for both owners and neighbors unless care is taken to ensure that it is kept within reasonable limits.

Some owners worry that if their puppy doesn't bark, it means that he will not make a good house dog when he gets older. Although this is a natural concern, it is unfounded, as many young puppies do not have enough confidence to bark at first. As their confidence grows, they will begin to raise the alarm if they perceive threats to the family and this usually begins in earnest at the age of about six to eight months.

Some puppies are more inclined to bark than others, terrier breeds in particular. If you allow or encourage your puppy to bark while he is still young, it is likely that he will do so too much once he reaches maturity. Excessive barking can easily become a self-rewarding habit that is difficult to break.

For this reason, it is best to interrupt barking as soon as it begins, or, better still, attract your puppy's attention just before it begins and engage him in an interesting activity on which he has to concentrate.

It is also important to actively discourage alarm barking by providing more fun in a different place so that your puppy does not learn to be worried about or try to scare off threats to the territory. Otherwise, this tendency may develop until it is difficult to contain once your puppy is older, stronger, and more confident.

BARKING ON COMMAND
It is best not to teach puppies to bark on command, unless you are an experienced trainer and can also stop them when necessary. Barking is a self-rewarding behavior and can quickly become a nuisance.

CORRECTIVE COLLARS

Never be tempted to use a collar that punishes your puppy with a citronella spray or electric shock whenever he barks. As well as frightening your puppy, the cause of his barking is still present and the desire to bark is still there. Since the situation is unresolved from your puppy's point of view, he may try other unwanted behavior instead.

EXCESSIVE BARKING

If your puppy barks more than you find comfortable, it is important to stop it early before it becomes an established habit. Puppies will bark for several different reasons: they could be fearful, excited, frustrated, bored or seeking attention. As well as interrupting the barking when it begins, it is also important to address the problem that is causing your puppy to bark.

TERRITORIAL BARKING

Some dogs, such as German shepherds, are particularly protective of their home and territory. This behavior is partially rooted in fear, and so it is very important to give them plenty of socialization and pleasant experiences with strangers so that they do not feel the need to keep them away. It is also important to give them plenty of opportunity to go to places away from home so that they get used to being out and about and so feel less attached to their home environment.

SOLVING THE PROBLEM

Fear/anxiety
• Remove your puppy or get farther away from whatever is causing the fear.
• Help your puppy to get used to whatever he is afraid of gradually, going at his speed, and providing tasty treats and games to help him have fun instead.

Excitement
• Provide more fun throughout the day to prevent one event from becoming too exciting.
• Keep still and allow the excitement to subside until the barking stops.
• Distract your puppy and get him to concentrate on something else instead.

Frustration and attention-seeking
• See pages 66–67.

Boredom
• Give your puppy more things to do and play with/train your puppy more.
• Give him more exercise/stimulation away from the home environment.

Walking on a loose lead with distractions

Walking nicely on a loose lead is the most difficult of the exercises for you and your puppy to master. By this stage, you should have a puppy who is practiced at trying to keep the lead loose when you walk. If not, go back to the previous stages and try again. Now it is time to teach him to do this whatever is going on around him.

Now that your puppy is staying close to you wherever you go and you no longer need to tell him that you are about to turn, practice this exercise in places where there are more distractions that your puppy may wish to investigate. Stop and reposition him if the lead goes tight and try to keep moving at a reasonably quick pace so that you remain more interesting than the other things around him. If your puppy is so interested in the distraction that you cannot get his attention, move away and try again, moving closer only once you have control.

WALKING PAST OTHER DOGS

Other dogs can be a big distraction for your puppy and it is likely that he will forget all about his lead training and pull hard to get to them. This is quite natural, and to overcome it, you will need to teach him how to walk well on the lead while other dogs are close by.

If you can, set up situations with friends who have dogs so that you can practice. Your friends' dogs will be more controllable than those loose on walks. Keep your distance from them and practice teaching your puppy to walk nicely on a loose lead. As he improves, gradually get closer to them. Work hard at being encouraging and interesting so that you are more rewarding than the dog in the distance.

Stop frequently and offer good rewards for walking nicely with you. If your puppy gets too interested in the other dog and he pulls on the lead, stop, stand still, and wait until the excitement has died down before repositioning him and rewarding him for being beside you. If you cannot get your puppy's attention, move farther away from the other dog and try again.

When you first begin to teach this exercise, ask the other owners to keep their dogs still. When you get more experienced, ask them to get their dogs moving. You will have full control when your puppy will walk nicely on a loose lead next to another dog that is playing and running.

PUPPIES AND LIVESTOCK

It is a good idea to get your puppy used to livestock, even if you live in a town, as you may relocate or have vacations in the countryside. Treat all encounters with livestock as a training opportunity, and teach your puppy how to walk on a loose lead around them.

RANDOM REWARDS

Once your puppy is walking nicely on a loose lead wherever you go and whatever is around you, it is time to begin to reduce the rewards he is getting and introduce jackpots (see page 74). Remember to save the rewards for good performances and the jackpots for exceptional performances, so that your puppy will behave well more frequently.

WALKING WITH OTHERS

Try not to be too disappointed if your puppy usually walks perfectly on the lead, but then behaves like an untrained dog when you begin walking with others. Walking with other dogs and people, particularly children, increases the excitement of a walk and will make it more difficult for your puppy to settle down enough to walk nicely on the lead without pulling.

You will need to treat these walks as a training session, stopping every time the lead goes tight, encouraging your puppy back to you, and rewarding him for doing so. This can be difficult if you are trying to keep up with a group, so it is better if you can get together with friends especially for the purpose of training and teach your puppy to walk well with others while you have time to do so.

When walking past people in the street, keep your puppy's attention focused on you. After they have passed him, reward him well for staying with you.

Wait—while the owner moves away

You have laid the foundation for this exercise during the last step and it is now time to build on this. Once you have taught your puppy to stay still while you move away, you can progress to asking him to wait regardless of whatever is happening around him.

Now that your puppy has learned to wait while you stand next to him, the next step is to teach him to keep still while you move away from him.

Once he has mastered the basic exercise, gradually build up until you can move all around him, walk farther away from him, and ask him to wait for longer periods. If he moves when you are at a distance, go back to him and gently put him back into position, then move away again before going back and rewarding him.

Once your puppy is happy to have you move away slowly and walk all around him, try moving away more quickly, slowly building this up until he is happy to sit still while you run away.

1 Get your puppy to sit by your side and get his attention.

2 Ask him to wait and give your hand signal.

3 Then slowly move one step to the side. If he moves, use the lead to keep him from moving too far and use a food lure to get him back into position. Don't feed the treat, but move away from him again.

TIPS FOR SUCCESS

• Remember to teach this exercise when your puppy is well exercised rather than energetic.

• Never ask your puppy to wait off the lead in a place near traffic or while you go out of sight.

• If your puppy moves several times during the training session, you are moving too far away too quickly and need to go back a few stages.

• Reward your puppy while he is in the sitting position more often than calling him to come to you from his sit position. Otherwise he may begin to anticipate being released, and it will become very difficult to keep him sitting still.

LYING DOWN

After your puppy has learned how to wait in a sitting position while you move away, teach the exercise again, but with him lying down instead. You will need to go back to the beginning again, but this time you should be able to progress more quickly, as your puppy will already have some understanding of what is required.

4 Reward him while he remains in that position.

IN A GOOD MOOD

Training a puppy is not always easy and can be very frustrating if you cannot get your puppy to understand what you want him to do. Plenty of patience is needed. If you are tired or unhappy before beginning your training, it is easy to become frustrated and angry.

Getting angry during a training session will confuse and frighten your puppy and may put him off further training sessions. Even if you try not to show it, your puppy will pick up the signals from your body language and the tone of your voice and will feel the pressure. So rest if you are tired or stressed and train when you are in a better mood instead.

If you are in the middle of a training session and feel yourself getting angry, ask your puppy to do something you know he can do, reward him well to make both of you feel better, and then end the training session.

Finding a training class

Finding good training classes takes time and energy, but it will be well worth it in terms of the good-quality information that they can provide. The difference between a good and bad class is immense and can make all the difference to your puppy and your willingness to continue further.

A good puppy training and socialization class will encourage you with your own training, teaching you the skills and techniques needed to train your puppy effectively. It will also help with any problems that you may encounter along the way. In addition, it will give your puppy the chance to meet and socialize with other puppies, children, and adults. Classes vary in quality, so select carefully from those available.

Go only to classes that use reward-based methods in a friendly, easy-to-learn environment. Avoid those where choke chains or force is used and where the mood is humiliating or chaotic. Ask for recommendations from friends, family, and veterinary staff, and try to visit a few classes so that you can choose the best. Go along without your puppy at first to see what the training is like. Avoid any classes that will not allow you to do so.

STRUCTURED LEARNING

Try to find a tutor who runs a set of classes with a start and finish rather than a rolling program where anyone can join at any time. This will give you a structured course and your puppy will get to know others in the class, which will help him to overcome any shyness and make friends. Ask what the tutor intends to cover before the course begins so that your expectations of what the course will give you will match what the course can deliver.

APPROPRIATE CLASSES

Be sure to find a class where all the puppies are of a similar age. Do not be tempted to take a very young puppy to a class where there are many adult dogs in a small area, as this may overwhelm your puppy and cause him to become fearful and defensive. Try to find a class where there is an age limit, for example a class for puppies up to twenty weeks, so that your puppy will not feel intimidated by others.

CORRECTIVE ACTION

If your puppy has a behavioral problem, you will need to find someone who has an in-depth understanding of dog behavior. They need to have been working with dogs for many years to gain the necessary experience, so check their work history carefully. A recommendation from someone who has tried out their methods or a referral from a vet is often the best way to find the right person. Also, they should be using only effective, humane methods, so avoid anyone who offers quick fixes in the form of aversion or punishment.

SUPERVISED BEHAVIOR

Although it is nice to see puppies playing together, a free-for-all where all the puppies are allowed to play together for a long period of time can create behavior problems with other dogs later in life. Unsupervised, unregulated play can cause some puppies to become fearful of others and they may quickly learn to use aggression to keep others away. In other cases, some strong players or puppies that bite hard may learn to enjoy playing roughly and bully others. Consequently, it is important to find a class where puppies are carefully chosen to play together, where only a few puppies are allowed off lead at once, and where all play is well supervised and controlled.

Problem solver

Some puppies take a long time to learn to trust humans and may find it more difficult than others to accept being handled. Others may have specific concerns about being touched in certain places.

Problem 1
My puppy doesn't like being touched.

• Practice gently holding the paws at first. If this is difficult, start at the elbow and gradually work down. If your puppy tries to pull his foot away when you reach the paw, hold on gently but firmly so that he cannot get it free. Keep him interested in a tasty treat while you do this to take his mind off it. As soon as he relaxes and lets you hold his paw, feed the treat, give lots of praise, and let the paw go.

• Continue until he is happy for you to hold any of his paws for as long as you wish, then over several sessions, gradually get him used to having his paws gently squeezed.

• Go at his speed, progressing over many sessions so that he learns to trust that you will not hurt him and is happy to accept whatever you do to him.

Problem 2
My puppy doesn't like his nails being clipped.

• Ask an experienced vet or nurse to show you how to clip your puppy's nails correctly. If you know how to do this properly, there is less risk that you will hurt your puppy in the process.

• Go slower and be more gentle. Paws are sensitive and care needs to be taken to get him to accept this gradually. Once you can handle his paws with ease (see Problem 1), get him used to having his toes gently spread apart, and his paws held as you would if you were going to cut his nails.

• When he is comfortable with this, accustom him to having the clippers placed slowly against one of his nails. Reward him well for accepting this and repeat for all the nails on each of his paws.

Problem 3
My puppy bites and struggles when held.

All puppies find it difficult to accept restraint at first. If you are gentle but firm with him, he will learn to accept it with time.

• Find a way to hold your puppy firmly but gently so that he cannot bite you, and then hold on.

• Let him wriggle and struggle all he likes, but wait until he has finished and relaxes. Then praise him and let him go.

• Pick him up often and hold him so that he quickly learns that the only way to be released is to relax and accept the restraint.

• Once he relaxes instantly, begin to hold him for increasingly longer times, talking calmly to him as you do so.

ARE YOU READY FOR THE NEXT STAGE?

Does your puppy sit when you give a voice cue in any location?

Does your puppy stand when you give a voice cue in any location?

Does your puppy lie down when you give a voice cue in any location?

Will your puppy come back from any distraction when you call?

Will your puppy come back from things he would like to chase when you call?

Is your puppy happy to be placed on a table and be examined by you (or a stranger) in the same way as a veterinary surgeon would?

Does your puppy relax and let you handle his paws in a way that would allow you to clip his nails easily?

Are you remembering to reward your puppy for walking well on a loose lead with occasional treats and jackpots?

Will your puppy stay in a sitting position while you count to twenty after you have moved four paces away from him?

Will your puppy stay in a down position while you count to twenty after you have moved four paces away from him?

Walking beside you without a lead

Now that your puppy is happy to walk beside you wherever you go while on a lead, it should be very easy to teach him to walk beside you without one.

Since you do not have a lead to keep him from leaving you, try to predict when he may begin to go toward the distraction and work hard to keep his interest on you at those times. Reward him well for staying with you when he would rather be elsewhere.

Continue, over several sessions, until your puppy stays walking with you even though there are interesting things going on around you. Then begin to reward randomly and with jackpots.

1 Find a quiet, safe place in which to work on this exercise where your puppy will not be distracted. Get his attention, show him that you have the treat, and ask him to walk next to you.

2 Walk a few paces before rewarding him. Since this exercise is essentially the same as the one you did during Walking on a Loose Lead (see page 68) but without the lead, your puppy should learn this easily. Put in a few turns and walk at different speeds to keep it interesting, but get your puppy's attention just before you intend to do something different so that he can stay with you. Make it clear when you have finished the exercise by rewarding him and telling your puppy that he can go free. Gradually build up this exercise, slowly introducing distractions and then getting closer to things that may cause your puppy to lose concentration.

HIGH ACHIEVERS

If you complete all the training exercises given in this book, your puppy will be trained to a very high standard compared with the majority of pet dogs. Teaching your puppy to this level will make it possible to take him out and about more easily. Since he will be well behaved and responsive, he will be more acceptable to those people who are not keen on dogs, and he will be able to be taken to more places, having a happier, more active life as a result.

The training in this book will give you a good foundation for further training should you want to continue. You may want to try some of the activities that involve dogs, such as working trials or obedience competitions. Many of these require jumping and so therefore cannot be attempted until your puppy is eighteen months old. Teaching your puppy the basic exercises in this book and teaching them well will give you the perfect platform for further activities with your dog, and he will be able to learn the new disciplines very easily.

Although you can teach old dogs new tricks, things learned during puppyhood stay with them for a lifetime, and it is much easier and quicker to teach them while they are young and receptive.

LEARNING TO UNDERSTAND WORDS

Many pet dogs are not trained well, and as a consequence, owners are often frustrated with them and punish them for not responding, even though the dog may not fully understand what is required. Dogs learn to gauge our moods from our body language and tone of voice, and this often causes people to assume that they understand much of our spoken language too. However, dogs cannot learn our vocabulary and are able to understand the meanings of only certain words that have been carefully taught to them. For this reason, the exercises in this book are designed to teach puppies all the essential words they need to know to make them easy to live with.

Waiting with distractions

Now that your puppy will stay still while you move around him in a quiet place, it is time to teach him to stay still when there are interesting things going on around him that he would rather get up to investigate.

Begin this process at a distance from something he is interested in and use a lead or long line to prevent him from running off should he decide to do so. Work with him carefully, teaching him to stay still whatever is going on and then getting steadily closer to the source of interest.

Gradually build up your puppy's tolerance of sitting still when he would rather be doing something else, giving him valuable rewards for doing so and letting him free, eventually, to play and investigate once he has been good for a short time.

If your puppy finds the distractions too exciting, try the same exercise farther away or find a place where there are less interesting things going on. Play more with your puppy beforehand so that he is happy to rest.

CAUTION
Never leave your puppy waiting in a place where he may be harmed if he gets up and walks off, such as near a road or outside a store.

ONE STEP FURTHER

If you want to take the "wait" further, you can teach your puppy to stay still while you go out of sight. Practice at home to begin with, asking your puppy to wait while you go into another room. Walk straight back in and reward him well. Gradually build up the time he will wait and then try again in different rooms of the house and also in the yard or park. Do not try this with young or shy puppies as they may not have enough confidence to stay in a room without you.

As he begins to become reliable, you can apply this lesson to real-life situations, such as waiting in the car. When you open the door, signal for him to wait. When you want him to come out of the car, give him the signal that he is now allowed out.

TIPS FOR SUCCESS

• Play an exciting game first so that your puppy will find it easy to keep still.

• Don't ask your puppy to wait for too long at first; build up the time gradually.

• Remember to give one voice cue only and make sure that your puppy responds. Do not get into the habit of continuously repeating the voice cue or hand signal in an effort to keep your puppy still. If he will not sit still, practice again farther away from the distraction and go back to the early lessons again until he is more reliable.

HOW MUCH TRAINING IS NEEDED?

For your puppy to be reliable about responding to requests, he must know what they mean and know that the rewards for complying outweigh the alternatives, whatever he is doing.

Regular, successful practice often throughout the day for six weeks will teach your puppy what the words and signals mean. You will then have to practice in different situations and with distractions going on around you for a further six weeks to make your puppy reliable.

Since you are teaching all exercises together and not just concentrating on one, the training process for all words and signals will take up most of your puppy's first year.

Tricks

Tricks are a good way to test your understanding of reward-based training and to give your puppy fun ways to exercise his mind.

Tricks can be useful or just amusing. Figure out a way to encourage your puppy to show the behavior you want so that you can reward it. Once your puppy is doing what you want every time, move to a different location and repeat. Put the trick on hand signal, then voice cue. Then begin to reward at random, saving occasional jackpots for very good performances.

> **IMPORTANT**
> Never teach your puppy to do anything that is demeaning or dangerous.

WAVE
The "wave" is an easy trick to teach and a good place to start trick training before becoming more ambitious.

1 Begin by holding a tasty treat near your puppy's paw. Resist all his attempts to lick and chew it out of your fingers and wait until he tries to scratch it out with his paw. As soon as his paw makes contact with your hand, feed the treat. Repeat many times over several sessions until your puppy will paw at your hand to get the treat. Once your puppy is happily raising his paw to get the treat, put in the voice cue "wave" just before you offer the treat.

2 Gradually begin to lift the treat higher. Wait until your puppy lifts and brings his paw up before feeding him the treat, and remember to feed him immediately when you get the desired response. Don't forget to add the voice cue each time just before you offer the treat.

3 Continue to raise the treat gradually until your puppy is happy to put his paw up to head height. After a few successful attempts at this, try raising the tidbit above his head and asking for a "wave." It will now be difficult for your puppy to figure out what is required as he can no longer touch your hand with his paw, so give him a few moments and wait. If he doesn't attempt to wave, lower your hand to his nose level, reward his paw lift, and then try again until he gets the idea. Ignore any jumping and reposition him if necessary.

4 Eventually, your puppy will "wave" when you hold up the treat and give the voice cue. If you want to, you can eventually reduce the hand signal until your puppy will "wave" when asked.

ROLLOVER

The rollover is a useful trick for when you want to examine the underside of your puppy.

1 Before attempting this trick, make sure that your puppy has a good, reliable response to the "down" command. From a "down" position, lure his head around to the side using a treat held right up against his nose. Try to place your hand in the position shown here so that it is easy to move it around farther later. Feed the treat in this position several times before moving on.

2 Moving very slowly, bring your puppy's head farther around to the side. Move your hand very slowly so that he has time to relax. If you are finding it difficult to keep his attention, use a big treat and allow him to chew little bits off to keep him interested. As he relaxes, he should begin to fall to the side while turning his head. Feed the treat and repeat several times over several sessions. Begin to add the voice cue "rollover" just before you ask him to roll on to his side.

3 Once he is comfortable with lying on his side, lure his head around slowly so that he begins to turn upside down. Reward him well with the treat and lots of praise as soon as he lies on his back. Remember to give the voice cue before you ask him to roll.

PERSEVERE

If your puppy won't do what he is supposed to, stop and think how you can proceed.

Break the trick down into very small steps and practice each one with your puppy before putting them together. Think how you can position the food lure to encourage your puppy to do each step.

4 When he is happy to roll on to his back, lure his head over so that he rolls on to his other side.

TIPS FOR SUCCESS

• If your puppy gets up, patiently ask him to lie down again and move your hand more slowly, carefully positioning the treat so that he doesn't think he needs to get up to reach it.

• You may find that puppies with thin coats or bony backs roll more easily on a soft blanket or carpet rather than a hard floor.

• The rollover is a vulnerable position and your puppy will be reluctant to take it up unless he feels completely safe. Practice at home when there are no other dogs or children present and ask for it only in places where he feels secure.

• Narrow, deep-chested dogs may find it difficult to adopt the position of lying on their backs, as they naturally fall to one side. This means that they may be reluctant to try it in case they get the sensation of their bodies moving without their control. If this is the case with your dog, help him by placing him on a thick, squashy pad that will support him a little before he tries this.

5 Continue until he has rolled all the way over and reward him well for doing so.

BREAKING DIFFICULT TRICKS
Break long or difficult tricks down into small steps.

If you break tricks down into steps, begin by teaching the last step first and practice until your puppy can do that part of the trick well. Then teach the step before that and put them together so that your puppy is moving on to something he knows how to do well.

WALK THROUGH A HOOP

"Walk through a hoop" is the precursor to more difficult tricks that involve jumping. This is a good trick to practice with your puppy if he is still too young to try more advanced tricks.

1 Position your puppy so that he is on the other side of the hoop to the hand containing the treat. (It may be easier to get someone to hold the hoop for you.)

2 Lure your puppy through the hoop, rewarding him well with the treat and praise once he steps through it.

3 Once he is going through it happily, position your puppy farther away (ask him to sit and stay or ask someone to hold him). Then call him through the hoop.

Later, when your puppy is mature and his bones and joints are fully formed, you can begin to raise the hoop so that, eventually, he learns to jump through it. Raise it slowly at first so that he can still step through it, and then increase the excitement and activity level, and then the height of the hoop, until he is jumping through.

WALK BACKWARD

"Walk backward" is a useful exercise for your puppy to learn. Try it when he is crowding you or if he is in a confined space and needs to move backward.

TIP FOR SUCCESS

• Keep your hand and its movement very straight so that he moves backward in a straight line. If he curves around, reposition him, move your hand more slowly, and try again.

1 Begin by holding the treat against your puppy's nose and bringing your hand down underneath his chin.

2 Gently move the treat backward (don't push against your puppy; position the treat so that he follows it instead). When he has moved just one paw backward, reward him immediately with a treat and praise.

Once he begins to get the idea, try for more than one step before rewarding him. Then give the voice cue just before you create the action and continue to practice in the usual way until he will move backward on cue until asked to stop.

"GO TO . . ."

"Go to . . ." can be a fun trick, with your puppy acting as a messenger. Reward him well and he will quickly begin to love his new job.

1 Hold your puppy by the collar and ask your helper to show your puppy that she has a treat.

2 Ask your helper to move backwards, then point in her direction, say "go to . . ." and release your puppy.

3 Your helper should reward your puppy well with a treat and praise when he gets to her.

Repeat a few more times and then ask your helper to run out of sight, sending your puppy to find her. Repeat the exercise over several sessions in different places until your puppy will happily run to your named person wherever they are in the house.

Once your puppy can find a named person, repeat the exercise with another person until he begins to understand the difference between the two names (this is quite difficult for your puppy to learn, so he will need lots of practice). Make sure that only the named person rewards the puppy so that he learns to try to find the correct person. If you teach this trick well, and your puppy learns the names of the people he lives with, he can act as a messenger by carrying notes in his collar. Make sure that he is always rewarded well for his efforts in order to maintain his enthusiasm.

SHUT THE DOOR

This trick is quite difficult, so work in short sessions and review what your puppy has learned at the end of each session, adjusting the training if necessary.

1 Teach your puppy to touch a target stick with his nose. A target stick can be anything that has an end and a handle. Keep it hidden, then present it to your puppy.

2 He will sniff at the new object and as soon as he touches the end with his nose, remove the target stick and quickly give him a treat and lots of praise as you do so. Repeat over several sessions until he will run to touch the target stick with his nose wherever it is placed.

3 Arrange for your puppy to wait near the door, then produce the target stick, putting it at nose height against the door. Reward your puppy well for touching it with his nose. Continue until your puppy will do this reliably, then begin to give the voice cue "shut the door" just before presenting the target stick. Then open the door a little and repeat. Once he is doing this well, generate excitement before presenting the target stick so that he runs forward, causing him to push the door instead and reward him well when the door closes.

Over time, open the door farther and reward harder pushes. Then remove the target stick and give only the voice cue. Wait to see if he understands, and help him with the target stick if need be. Eventually, you should be able to ask him from a distance to do this and then return to you for his reward.

RETRIEVE

The "retrieve" forms the basis of many tricks and more advanced training, and shouldn't be rushed or forced. Most puppies will retrieve naturally and we just need to tap into their instinctive desire to hold and possess objects. It is important not to get upset or scold your puppy while teaching this exercise—all his associations with toys, objects, and you should be happy ones.

Remember that control reduces enthusiasm. Get him enthusiastic about the game of retrieve first before you get too controlling about your puppy returning to you with the toy. Control can always be added later.

DIFFERENT PLACES
Remember to practice in different places and situations and in more distracting circumstances once your puppy has learned the trick so that he knows how to do it anywhere.

Don't scold your puppy for doing the wrong thing, as this will put him off. Just reward the action you want and keep trying different ways to get him to do it until you are successful.

1 Generate plenty of excitement by teasing your puppy with his favorite toy for a short time.

2 Roll the toy away from you, encouraging your puppy to follow by saying "fetch it" in an exciting way.

3 Stand in the place where you think your puppy will return and encourage him to come to you once he has picked up the object.

TIPS FOR SUCCESS

• Never play until your puppy is exhausted. Throw the toy several times and then play a different game.

• While your puppy is still young, keep the distance that you throw the toy short so that you do not overtire him or put too much strain on his growing joints.

• Before you try this exercise, your puppy needs to be very interested in playing with toys. If he is not, see Step 1 for ways to develop this.

• If your puppy is already trying to avoid you, as you have taken his toys away in the past, attach a line to his collar and use this to teach him that you will not take his toy if he returns to you.

• If your puppy prefers to play tug-of-war rather than chase, encourage him to come back to you and, rather than taking his toy, encourage him to play tug-of-war instead to reward him for coming back to you. When you are ready to ask him to let go, hold the toy tightly against you so that he cannot tug and wait until he lets go.

• If your puppy lies down in a place away from you rather than coming to you, go and sit in that place next time so that he comes back to you when he goes there.

• If your puppy runs after the toy, but does not pick it up, choose a softer, lighter toy that is easier to bite.

4 Praise him and make a big fuss of him when he returns. DO NOT take his toy away at once or he will begin to avoid returning to you. Instead, stroke his body and tell him how pleased you are with him. When he begins to mouth the toy and looks as though he may be getting ready to drop it, take it gently from his mouth, holding on to the toy firmly against you so that the game cannot turn into a tug-of-war, and repeat the whole sequence.

MORE RETRIEVE EXERCISES
Once your puppy can do this exercise, you can teach him all sorts of retrieve tricks such as:
• Fetch slippers
• Fetch the remote control
• Fetch the newspaper
• Fetch a toy

Continue to practice in different places, with different objects, and, later, with stationary objects, until he learns that "fetch it" means that he should pick up the object and bring it back.

FIND A HIDDEN TOY

Once your puppy is happy to retrieve toys, you can move on to teaching him to find hidden objects. Once he has learned this lesson, you can send him to find objects hidden around the house; this will keep him occupied for a long time and use up his mental energy.

VOICE CUES

Start to give the voice cue once your puppy is repeatedly doing part of the required action. Say the word just before you position the food lure so that your puppy learns to associate the word with the action.

1 Let your puppy watch while someone hides his favorite toy under a blanket. In the early stages, leave a bit uncovered so that it can be seen.

2 Point it out to him and send him to find and retrieve it.

3 Reward him well and play a short game with him when he brings the toy back.

TIPS FOR SUCCESS

• Check to make sure that he is being successful, and if you think he is struggling to find the hidden object, help him out. As he begins to learn and develop his skills, he will need less help, but always make sure that he is successful.

• If your puppy is more interested in food than toys, hide a toy that contains food to give him more incentive to find it.

4 After several repetitions, hide the toy completely in the blanket so that he has to search for it.

5 When he successfully finds the toy, again reward him by playing with him with the toy he has found.

Once he has gotten the idea, you can begin to increase the complexity of the search, hiding things in different places and, eventually, in different rooms in the house. Always go back to basics when you teach him to find a toy in a new place and make it easy for him to find it. If you want to teach your puppy to be really clever, teach him the names of different toys and send him to find each in turn.

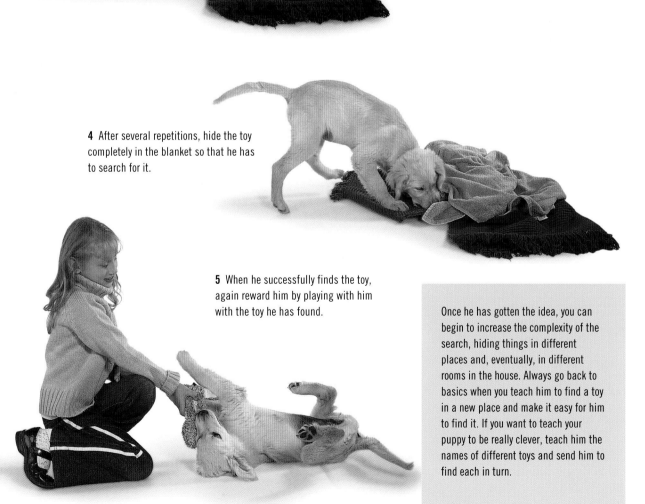

Adolescence

As with children, adolescence can be a time when all your hard work seems to have been wasted. However, just as teenagers grow up, puppies mature and become adults. Knowing what to expect and understanding that it will come to an end can really help during this difficult stage.

Puppies will reach maturity at different ages. Generally, smaller dogs mature faster and are usually adults by about twelve months of age. Larger dogs can take longer and may take eighteen to twenty-four months before they mature fully.

This difference means that puberty is reached at different ages. At puberty, sex hormones begin to circulate and a puppy's focus of attention begins to shift to the outside world. In addition, their confidence develops and they are more exploratory, preferring to roam farther from their home territory if allowed to do so. Puppies from small breeds usually reach puberty at five to six months, whereas it can take seven months to a year for the larger breeds.

Until puberty, a puppy will rely on his owner to protect him and provide for his needs, and so will spend a lot of time strengthening his bond with his owner and will be very responsive and compliant.

THE TERRIBLE TEENS

When a puppy reaches puberty, his attention begins to turn to the wider world around him and away from his owners. This can be upsetting and frustrating for owners who were, until recently, the center of their puppy's world. During this time, problems with recall and attention are common, as it will become more difficult to distract your puppy from things such as scents on the ground and other dogs.

It is important to realize that this is just a difficult phase that all puppies go through, much like children go through a difficult teenage transition. Fortunately, once puppies become young adults, their behavior begins to improve and, eventually, returns to normal levels as they reach maturity.

Training your puppy while he was young means that you will already have put in place all the guidelines he needs to be well behaved. You just need to accept that he is going to be difficult for the next six months.

Keep up the training, use a long line to prevent him from running off if necessary, and wait for it all to come to an end. Try not to make requests unless you are in a position to ensure that your puppy complies. Eventually, this stage will pass, and because you have kept up the training, he will return to being well behaved and a delight to own.

CATCH THEM YOUNG

If you have just acquired an adolescent puppy or did not begin training until later, it is not too late. It will, however, be more difficult than training a very young puppy and you will have to work hard to keep his attention. Train him with exercises at home first where there are less distractions and then make use of a long line to ensure compliance when outside. It helps to accept that adolescent puppies are difficult to train, as this will help you to be more patient and not to get frustrated when you cannot get him to do what he is supposed to do.

INDEPENDENCE

Adolescent puppies like to explore and may try to get out of the garden unless it is securely fenced. If confined to the house, they may chew much more as a way of exploring their environment and may begin to chew things that they previously ignored. To counteract this, try to provide as much off-lead exercise in new places as possible, taking them on new walks and providing plenty of stimulation by going to different places. In addition, when they are at home, give them lots of different things to chew and explore, making changes frequently so that they are kept occupied and are therefore less likely to chew things they should not.

Congratulations!

If you have completed the puppy training course given in this book, you will now have a puppy who understands all the basic commands and is ready for life as a happy family pet.

Although there are many exercises to be done, completing the course will mean that your puppy is better trained than most dogs and will be much easier to live with. Since the methods are fun and enjoyable for you both, short sessions can be regularly fitted into your daily schedule so that your puppy can improve gradually as time passes and he moves into adulthood.

Lessons taught early in life are remembered more clearly that those taught later and so you will have laid an excellent foundation for the rest of your dog's life. However, dogs, like people, need to be reminded of their lessons from time to time, and if you continue to give short refresher sessions throughout his life, his response will stay sharp. As you expanded his mind when he was young, he will want to learn and will enjoy his training, and because you learned how to teach him using positive methods, teaching anything new should be a joy for you both.

Step 1 Early lessons Building a good relationship, setting boundaries, and starting well gave you the best chance of success during the training exercises given in the following chapters.

Step 2 Positive training Reward-based training allows you to teach important exercises, such as coming back when called. Early learning also involved getting to know different people and other dogs, as well as learning to be alone and traveling in the car.

Step 3 Essential exercises Important lessons for your puppy involved learning how to sit, stand, and lay down when asked, to come back on a walk, greeting people without jumping up, getting used to being handled, and learning not to be possessive over food, chews, and bones.

Step 4 Good practice The training was extended by teaching hand signals to help your puppy bridge the gap between being lured and the voice cue, as well as learning to walk on a loose lead, being handled by strangers and learning how to deal with frustration.

Step 5 Extra lessons Your puppy was gradually introduced to different-looking humans as well as being examined by strangers in preparation for the vet. As your puppy began to learn what was required, we introduced random rewards and jackpots to improve his responses.

Step 6 Further education As training progressed, responses to voice cue only were taught, as well as wait, coming back when your puppy would rather be doing something else, and walking on a loose lead when there were things present to distract him.

Step 7 Advanced training Finally, clever tricks were taught so that further fun could be had, as well as more advanced lessons such as learning to walk beside you without a lead.

HAVE YOU FINISHED THE COURSE?

• Will your puppy walk next to you off the lead in places where there are lots of things to interest him?

• Will your puppy wait when you ask, even though exciting things are going on around him?

• Can your puppy do a simple trick?

Positive training builds a happy partnership between you and your puppy that will last forever. This book has given you the techniques and knowledge needed to do it well. How much your puppy learns and how well educated he becomes is up to you. Training him during his puppyhood to a standard sufficient to allow him to be welcome anywhere will mean that both of you will get the best from your relationship and he will be a joy to own for the rest of his life.

Index

A
adolescence 21, 122–3
aggression 54, 80
alone, leaving puppy 34–5
animals 38, 99
anxiety, being left alone 34–5
associations, varying 63, 76–7
attention of puppy, getting 26–7
attention-seeking behavior 67, 73

B
backward, walking 115
barking 96–7
    attention-seeking 67
    being left alone 34, 35
    excessive barking 97
    preventing 72–3
    territorial barking 97
biting
    preventing play biting 10,
        12–13
    when being held 105
boisterousness 70–1
bonding
    with other dogs 15
    with owner 10–11; 23
bones, overprotectiveness 54–5
boredom
    barking 97
    varying treats 50
boundaries, setting 19

C
cages, travel 32
cars
    road safety 84–5
    travel in 32–3
car sickness 33
chasing 93
cheese, as treat 25
chewing 20–1
chews 20, 54–5
children, socializing puppy 14–15,
    37
classes 102–3

clipping coat 53
clipping nails 95, 104
coat
    clipping 53
    grooming 52
collars 24
    corrective collars 97
coming when called 28–9
    from something more interesting
        62–3, 92–3
    random rewards 74–5
    on walks 46–7, 56–7
commands see hand signals; voice
    cues
corrective collars 97

D
digging 72
discipline 19
dogs
    bonding with puppy 15
    socializing puppy 38–9
    walking past other dogs 98
doors
    front door etiquette 79
    scratching 34, 35
    "shut the door" trick 117
"down" 45
    hand signals 60–1
    voice cues 90–1
drying puppy 30

E
energetic puppies 70–1
environments, socializing puppy
    38, 39
exercise, lack of 70–1
eye contact 26

F
fat puppies 25
fears
    barking 97
    noise phobias 39
    of traffic 85
food
    begging for 15
    jumping up at table 59
    lures 43
    overprotectiveness 54–5
    as treat 25
front door etiquette 79

frustration 66–7

G
games
    look-at-me 26
    tail-wagging 26
garden, digging in 72
good manners 9
"go to" trick 116
grabbing puppy 53
greeting people see meeting
    people
groomers, preparing for visit to
    52–3
growling 80

H
hand signals 23, 43, 58–9
    different associations 76–7
    "down" 60–1
    "sit" 58
    "stand" 60–1
    "wait" 86, 87
handling puppy 29, 30–1
    biting 105
    dislike of being touched 104
    preparing for vet or groomer
        52–3
    by strangers 64–5
    on a table 94–5
    veterinary examinations 80–1
    while eating 55
hidden toys, finding 120–1
hoop, walking through 114
house-training 16–17, 22
hugging puppy 31

I
isolation 34–5

J
jackpots 75, 77, 99
jumping through a hoop 114
jumping up
    attention-seeking 67
    with children 88–9
    preventing 37, 48–9, 79
    at table 59

L
lead training 24
    letting puppy off lead 46–7

Acknowledgments

Author's acknowledgments
I would like to thank John Rogerson, who gave me such a good grounding in dog behavior and training that I still use it as a baseline today, and Tony Orchard, for giving me so many valuable tips on training. Thanks are also due to Kay and David Key and their little yappers and cats, for providing me with the space and encouragement necessary to write this book, to Trevor Davies, at Hamlyn, for wanting to publish it, and to Helen Cleary, for tirelessly organizing all the puppies and owners for the photos.

I would also like to thank John and Lea Hoerner, for their untiring support and good advice during the setting up of Puppy School and also just for being there. The Puppy School tutors I've collected as a result have been fantastic and have taught me more than they realize, which has helped me write a better book than it would otherwise have been.

And finally, I could not have written this book and been optimistic about it being good, if it hadn't been for the countless dogs and owners I've practiced on, including my own now-deceased dogs Winnie, Beau, and Sammy, and, more recently, my lovely puppy Spider. I'm relieved that I always tried to perfect the art of positive techniques so that at least my mistakes were relatively harmless.

Publisher's acknowledgment
Mike Wheeler Motorcycles Ltd.
108–110 High Street,
Witney, Oxon, UK
Tel: 01993 702660

Picture acknowledgments
Special photography © Octopus Publishing Group Limited/Steve Gorton

Other photography
Octopus Publishing Group/Rosie Hyde 10 right, 39 bottom right, 107 bottom left

Executive editor Trevor Davies
Executive art editor Leigh Jones
Designer Tony Truscott and Colin Goody
Photographer Steve Gorton
Picture researcher Jennifer Veall
Production controller Manjit Sihra